DUNDEE
A SHORT HISTORY

DUNDEE
A SHORT HISTORY

NORMAN WATSON

BLACK & WHITE PUBLISHING

First published 2006
by Black & White Publishing Ltd
99 Giles Street, Edinburgh EH6 6BZ

Reprinted 2006

ISBN 10:   1 84502 115 0
ISBN 13:   978 1 84502 115 3

British Library Cataloguing in Publication Data:
A catalogue record for this book is available
from the British Library.

Printed and bound by Nørhaven Paperback A/S

CONTENTS

ACKNOWLEDGEMENTS

I am indebted to many people for help with this work, among them family, friends and colleagues who have supported my writing over many years. Shirley Blair scrutinised the text on my behalf and I thank her, once again, for her diligence and guidance. D. C. Thomson & Co Ltd, as ever, were exceptionally helpful.

Special thanks are due to professional staff in a number of institutions. Eileen Moran, Deirdre Sweeney and colleagues at the Local Studies department of Dundee Central Libraries were unstinting in the help and guidance offered. Gwen Kissock and Anne Swadel of D. C. Thomson's archives department and Kay Beveridge lately of the firm's library provided cheery support, expertise and gossip along the way. I also offer thanks to Ian Flett and Richard Cullen of Dundee City Archives. Librarians at Forfar Library helpfully introduced me to the John C. Ewing bequest of historical books and documents. Staff at the rare books room at the British Library were helpful on numerous occasions. I also offer sincere thanks to Archie Duncan, Emeritus Professor of Scottish history and literature at the University of Glasgow, for permission to quote from his research on medieval Dundee. On this subject I congratulate the Scottish Urban Archaeology Trust (SUAT) for its pioneering excavations and monitoring work in Dundee.

Numerous published works were consulted for this history. If I have omitted to mention the contribution of any author I hope this note of gratitude will be acceptable. I also took the liberty of drawing on interviews I carried out for *The Courier* between 1981 and 2003. Specific publication references in the text have been avoided in the interest of readability, but all sources are listed in the bibliography.

I am indebted to Black & White Publishing of Edinburgh and grateful for the encouragement of one of their leading writers, my friend and former colleague Alexander McGregor. Gordon Dow in Dundee remains an unsung star of the local book trade and his professional advice and support were also appreciated.

Finally, I am grateful for the inspirational help from those who shared their experiences and memories of Dundee with me.

INTRODUCTION

The British Library in London was the biggest building built in the UK in the twentieth century. Below its ground-level plaza, between Euston and St Pancras stations, lie nine floors of shelves containing virtually every printed title in Britain. But the unmissable attraction of this breathtaking building is the library's Treasures Room. Here are the Magna Carta, the Lindisfarne Gospels, Shakespeare's first folio, the desk on which Jane Austen wrote her novels and the lyrics to The Beatles' *Yesterday*.

Shining brightly in this firmament of printed stars is the ancient hand-drawn map of Great Britain by the medieval monk Matthew Paris. Completed around 1250, it is a sumptuous treasure. This is the best of early British maps, one of the oldest in Europe and it is a miracle that it has survived. In bold letters, in its precise geographical location, is 'Dunde'. It is one of only a handful of correctly-located communities and hints at a settlement of importance by the early thirteenth century – a poke in the eye for neighbouring but absent Perth, which has agitated over historical precedence from then till now. Alas, the map probably acted as a tour guide for Edward I's army which spilled over the border and ransacked Dundee, almost before its ink had dried.

The god of geography smiled on Dundee's stunning location, but it is a mite unnerving in today's citadel of journalists that the spelling of the town's name has taken so many forms . . . Dunde by the bloodthirsty English, Dondei by Mary, Queen of Scots, Dundie by Bonnie Dundee and Dundy by a town clerk – possibly the inspiration for *The Dandy*, which chuckled its way out of D. C. Thomson in 1937. At the last count thirty-two variations of the name are known. The godly grin must be as wide as the estuary.

Divine intervention aside, where and when did Dundee begin? How do we separate the known from the unknown, the fact from fiction, and make sense of Dundee's beginnings? Unfortunately, history is annoyingly obscure about the city's origins. Only now and then is the curtain hiding its ancient past lifted, encouraging printed pot shots by local historians that are sometimes wide of the mark. Partly because of the silence of the sources, published histories lazily follow one another in cut-and-paste copying to locate the earliest settlement in the Seagate. Archaeological evidence and analysis of the burgh's earliest charters suggest they are a couple of streets out. The true heart of early Dundee, a gathering place of genuine and considerable antiquity, is unearthed in Chapter One.

A gift from one brother to another is how Dundee comes down to us in the earliest surviving documentation. Chapter Two examines the development of the town under Earl David of Huntingdon – the prototype 'Dundonian' – and its growing influence as an administrative, economic and religious centre. It introduces the town's enigmatic links to William Wallace and its defining role in the Wars of Scottish Independence. It uses evidence from an ancient cemetery to reconstruct the lifestyles and living conditions of the town's medieval inhabitants – the healthy, happy inhabitants who set us along the road and the miles to Bonnie Dundee.

Always in the path of war, Dundee was sacked, retaken,

sacked and retaken in the blood-filled battles of the Anglo-Scottish wars. The struggle for the crown involved John Balliol and Robert the Bruce, two warrior kings whose roots in Dundee are far deeper than imagined, allowing Chapter Three to question Angus Council's claim for the county as the Birthplace of Scotland. But Dundee's road to burghal status was contested and controversial. The 1300s began with Edward I crushing the town and ended with the English leaving it a smoking ruin once again. Dundee then passed by descent into the ownership of two aristocratic women – enough to make patriarchal jute barons birl in their tombs. Perhaps the womanly touch contributed to the respite from invasion, commotion, pillage and pestilence in the 1400s – and the creation of the first familiar landmarks from our past, the harbour, the Steeple and Broughty Castle. The Dundee of today was taking shape.

Dundee's evolution into a prosperous medieval burgh is one focus of Chapter Four. Under the brooding umbrella of the Sidlaws, every outlying hamlet had a weaving industry and every cottage was a factory. Empowered by its peripheral bleach fields and proximity to the sea, medieval Dundee crossed the threshold from agricultural to exchange economy. Although only a single flax seed has been uncovered by archaeologists, the town became a centre for cloth production, fitting out the armies of Europe in a coarse cloth called plaid, dyed in different colours by different combatants to avoid 'friendly fire'. Textiles had taken hold of the town. Then, in an era when politics and religion thundered hand in hand across Scotland, the Dundee of the mid-1500s hijacked the Reformation. Buildings were destroyed and religious relics ripped out in episodes of iconoclastic bedlam. Worse was to follow. Come the 1600s, the town was uniquely attacked and destroyed by both sides of the English Civil Wars. Progress and prosperity were brutally interrupted. The community vacillated from privilege to poverty in the space of two decades. A hundred years of development was irrevocably set back. The people even took to burning witches again.

The 1700s began with the hangover of siege throbbing and the town's fragile economy affected by England's anti-Gallic prejudices after the Union of 1707. Dundee was occupied during the rebellions of 1715 and 1745, and its road to prosperity continued to be hampered and hindered. But just as it offered an inviting landing point for invaders, so the harbour was a wonderful conduit for trade – and Dundee was always better at commerce than combat. The scars of the seventeenth century repaired, it made a timely switch from cloth to linen and became, by the late 1700s, a town of ambitious, enterprising merchants, as radical in politics as it had been in religion. It launched its whaling and shipbuilding industries. New factories produced soap and sugar. There were tanning yards and an important thread industry: glimpses of these now-extinct trades survive in street names such as Whale Lane, Candle Lane and Sugar-House Wynd.

In an era of revolutionary thinking, pre-jute Dundee enjoyed its own 'enlightenment'. Grand civic buildings were erected and cultural societies thrived. This wonderful century is captured in Chapter Five which also brings to life some of the characters involved, not least the artful Alexander Riddoch, who coerced his way through a near half-century of autocratic rule as Dundee's oligarchal, indestructible, been-there-seen-it-done-it-all provost.

Entering the 1800s, Dundee harnessed steam power

technology and grew fat on linen profits. Chapter Six takes readers to the unassuming street which introduced power-mills, where rural weavers looked in wonder at machinery bearing the name-plates of Watt and Arkwright. Through their efforts, Dundee was transformed into Britain's leading importer of flax and exporter of linen. There was 'a buoyant spirit of intelligence, enterprise, assiduous labour and successful speculation'. Linen sales brought riches – but from where? Hitherto unexplored markets linked Dundee to the slave trade and this makes for uncomfortable reading.

'King Jute' was how the *Advertiser* headlined the pinnacle of Dundee textile production – the backbone of Chapter Seven. The arrogant palaces of the dynastic manufacturing families transformed Broughty Ferry into Britain's wealthiest suburb and saw more Rolls-Royces outside the town's skirt of exotic mansions than anywhere else in the country. Huge mills and factories became great industrial villages with their own housing, schools, churches and railway lines. Mill money built obelisks, bell towers and extravagant porticos in the fashion of ancient Greece and Rome, to reflect their owners' pride. Profits were ploughed into speculative American cattle ranch ventures – the equivalent of £250 million in one decade alone. But jute also brought a precipitous decline in living standards and left the working classes demoralised in appalling domestic surroundings. Dundee was Dickens' semi-mythical Coketown.

Jute by no means disappeared in the first half of the twentieth century, but Chapter Eight explains its decline. What did not change was the domestic drama played out in the city's seething alleys and wynds. Dundee had some of the worst slum conditions in Scotland, the 1917 Royal

Commission reporting 32,000 inhabitants in overcrowded conditions, sometimes eight or ten to a room. The transformation began in 1919 with Scotland's first housing scheme at Logie and the country's first Garden City suburb for working classes at Craigie. The new century also brought a watershed in the city's political landscape – the demise of the Victorian Liberal Party and the rise of Labour. It brought Winston Churchill and Ernest Shackleton to stand for election, and to face local politicians such as the Bible-thumping Neddy Scrymgeour, Britain's only Prohibitionist MP. The young Dundee men killed at the Battle of Loos – where twenty-one out of twenty-three officers in a single local battalion died alongside hundreds of their men – tore the heart out of the town. Survivors returned to find no work waiting and no reservoirs of alternative income. Mob riot – that symptom of the despondent unemployed – was never far below the surface.

The transmogrification of Dundee from industrial desert to cultural oasis is the focus of Chapter Nine. Post-war industrial dispersal saw NCR, Timex, Ferranti, Holo-Krome, Vidor and Burndept among big-hitting new employers. From a standing start of 182 jobs in the new industries in 1942, Dundee quickly boasted a workforce of 12,000 as jute hands swapped mill aprons for factory overalls, and spindles for circuit boards. Thousands followed the factories to the brave new world of indoor lavatories on vast housing estates along the Kingsway. By 1980, fifty high-rise blocks had replaced jute chimneys on the city's skyline. Into areas cleared of tenements grew Dundee's world-class centre for scientific research, notably the £12 million Wellcome Trust research centre on Hawkhill, a totem of the city's dynamism and future direction. Dundee also enjoyed a rapidly-growing reputation as a centre of educational excellence as two new universities brought the total of term-time students in town to 25,000. The Technology Park harnessed call centres, blue chip companies and leading-edge industries. The £250 million Overgate shopping centre led the way in the reinvigoration of Dundee's retail heart. The opening of Dundee Contemporary Arts in 1999 and the stunning success of Dundee Rep transformed the Perth Road area into a buzzing cultural quarter.

Chapter Ten puts the old and new into context – and it does not pull punches. While post-industrial Dundee has undergone a remarkable period of reinvention and increasing confidence, the problems with an image created through misjudgements of the city, which have dogged it since the era of jute dominance, have been slow to recede. The disagreeable sticking-plaster planning of the Waterfront and Tay road bridge landfall area, new riverside offices and harbour-side housing verging on the architecturally disappointing, imply problems waiting to be solved. For every quaint wynd there is an uncompromising office block. There is also the problem that Dundee remains a city eight miles by six. Its boundaries are still twanged like elastic by a territorially-acquisitive city council keen to maximise revenue by recovering areas lost in boundary changes.

Yet, as a community, Dundee has always been historically aware, strong in common sense, and determinedly keen to retain its identity and individuality. The final chapter challenges the stereotypical prejudices of mainstream Scottish thinking and plots a bright future for Scotland's sunniest city as it continues this amazing era of development and change.

1

1000BC TO AD1000
FIRST FOOTSTEPS

Dundee began . . . where? Refer to four centuries of local histories and the answer is the Seagate, the congested, dropping-off street behind Marks & Spencer. Or how about under the seat in City Square on which I am writing the opening lines of this latest history?

Account after account records that a community settled on the shoreline in the Seagate, living in mud and wattle huts and using the mighty river to come and go and as a source of food. Thus Dundee evolved from their first footprints on this God-given estuarial site. In the early 1990s, Glasgow University's emeritus professor of history Archie Duncan turned history on its head by showing that four centuries of historians were up the wrong dreel. They had mistranslated or mistranscribed an ancient charter. Instead, he showed that Dundee had developed around a market place between present-day High Street and City Square.

Recent archaeological evidence has supported Duncan's view. In 1993 an undocumented cemetery containing the earliest burgh burials was found beneath the fifteenth-century Steeple. Trial trenching at Gardyne's Land, opposite City Square, suggested occupancy on the site as early as the 1100s. Medieval timber buildings were found at an excavation at the junction of Murraygate and

Panmure Street. All the new evidence was leading away from Seagate by locating the burgh's beginnings in a line from the present-day Overgate to Wellgate. The alternative location is also supported by a charter stating that the river was still lapping the south side of Seagate in 1414. This, too, throws doubt on the tradition that the burgh began there and developed westwards – a claim logged in local history books from the eighteenth century on, including Small (1792), Chalmers (1842), McLaren (1847), Maxwell (1884), Lamb (1895), Millar (1925), Torrie (1990), Whatley (1993), Scott (1999) and onwards to Gillian Ferguson as recently as 2005.

As to why a community should have formed on this riverside site twelve miles from the sea, all you have to do is climb to the rounded summit of the vitrified Law, recover your breath, keep the brooding Sidlaws to your back, and view today's southerly skyline. You might imagine something of what a nomadic tribesman may have seen thousands of years ago. The Tay shimmers west to east, though narrower than long ago. The dual peaks of the Lomonds pierce the sublime southern panorama. The Carse of Gowrie spreads picturesquely to the west, while the estuary widens to eye-filling proportions on the eastern horizon, illuminating one of the finest seafronts in Scotland. It is a timeless, magnificent scene, a museum of nature's landscape. Now look down at the crescentic indent of estuarial coastline below. What incomparable and striking physical surroundings to site the first settlement – on a raised beach, in a south-facing sheltered bay, under hopeful skies looking outwardly to what lay beyond the sand-duned gates to the open sea.

With a harbour sheltered from every wind except the south, a fish-filled river met by two burns providing water for drinking and washing, the narrowest crossing point of the Firth of Tay to the south shore on the important eastern route through Scotland, shielded by a range of low hills, a fertile hinterland offering potential for food and trade – the picture-perfect site of modern Dundee was stunningly positioned to be occupied, settled and founded from the earliest times.

In ancient topography the water of the Tay lapped the shore along the line of the Seagate to a hill later to be fortified and known as Castlehill. The shore then continued west to roughly the site of Tay Bridge Station, where another promontory, St Nicholas Craig, jutting out into the river, helped shape a natural harbour. Inland the lie of the land was broken by an outcrop of solid rock called Corbie Hill, which marked the road west. These three hills were later gouged out to allow for Castle Street, Whitehall Street and North Lindsay Street. Beyond the shore, Balgay Hill, Hawkhill and Hilltown were larger protuberances. To the north, between present-day Ward Road and Wellgate, an area of marshland stretched to the lower slopes of the extinct volcano, Dundee Law.

It was prehistoric people who unconsciously laid down the boundaries of the modern city. Subterranean buildings discovered on Balgay Hill and near Camperdown House are thought to have been storage structures, or protective winter dwellings for the earliest local inhabitants. A Stone Age shellfish midden, superimposed with Bronze Age pottery, was discovered in the Stannergate in 1878, and a crematory urn found in Perth Road in 1881. At Pyotdykes, north of Dundee, archaeologists in 1963 excavated a native British bronze spearhead with a gold band, and two bronze swords, lost or left some 6,000 years ago. Earth houses spanning many centuries and

Iron Age forts followed, then evidence of the first timber structures, providing landmarks of organised activity in the city confines. Virtually no documentary evidence has survived from these Dark Ages of Dundee, but tantalising local finds suggest very early and continuous occupation.

Mutual protection and self-interest led to clusters; clusters grew and commanded respect; inhabitants were granted security by local landlords or warlords in return for support and influence; laws were formed for the common good and trade was enabled. The Greek chronicler Ptolemy referred to the area as home to some of the Taezali tribe when he wrote of his travels around AD142 – though the area was probably occupied and contested by a loose confederation of quarrelsome families, doubtless flaunting rival tangerine and dark blue woad.

Agricola, who served as an able if acquisitive Roman governor of the British Isles between AD78 and 85, advanced to the Tay without formidable opposition, as his biographer Tacitus recorded in AD97. 'The enemy durst not meet him in the field, and no pitched battle was fought; but his army was greatly distressed with the severities of the climate.' Much later, when the Tangerines and Dark Blues achieved the pinnacle of their own history, the European Cup semi-finals, climatic complaints were again made within earshot by their Italian visitors.

It is probable that Agricola's army marched via the Sidlaws to the Carse of Gowrie, while the ships of his northern fleet, which held around 4000 men, may have anchored in the Firth of Tay. Excavations on Dundee Law in 1993 revealed a Roman rectangular enclosure surrounded by a rampart. That there is no substantive evidence of Roman activity in the vicinity of today's city centre is probably due to its site being open and overlooked from the north, and doubtless difficult to defend.

The Romans in Scotland were militaristic aggressors, not town-builders. On the other hand, the occasional discovery of coin hordes suggests considerable movement and trade in the region. The presence of an Imperial bronze Greek coin beneath a Tullideph Road drying green in 1969 is harder to explain.

After Agricola's governorship ended, the fort-building era also passed and the impetus of Roman conquest and occupation faded. The void in history between the Roman evacuation of Scotland in the 300s and the Pictish world of the fifth to ninth centuries continues Dundee's Dark Ages, seducing local histories into dismissing the period in a meagre quota of words. Evidence of post-Roman life and settlement near the Tay is shrouded in the mists of time, leaving future historians to wonder what was going on. Symbolic metalwork and sculpted stones apart, little remains of early Christianity's mission to the Picts after the legions had vanished. But Romanised travellers would have joined this settlement of self-sufficient people and engaged it in conversation or combat over territory, material goods and personal relationships. In the sixth century St Columba is said to have referred to his missionary work with the 'tribes of the Tay'. Could this saintly intercession have taken place near the modern city?

Neither would the evolving Dundee have been isolated from the push-and-shove Pictish civil war, which broke out in the year of 724, according to fairly reliable Irish chronicles. In 834 the area supposedly fell under the rule of King Alpin, King of the Scots. North of the Tay lay the lands of his bitter enemies, the Picts, in all probability the Caledonii of Roman authors. Brude, King of the Picts, less than pleased at the presence of the Scots in his backyard, brought his troops south to the Sidlaws. In the inevitable meeting of angry young kings, Alpin was defeated near King's Cross Road in Dundee, where his decapitated body is reputedly buried. Rape-and-pillage incursions by seaborne marauders would have also touched upon the estuary within easy sight of the fearful inhabitants of pre-urban Dundee. The Danes who chose to land near Carnoustie in 1010 were met and defeated at Barrie by the Scots under Malcolm II, who is said to have assembled his army in Dundee. We cannot say for certain if this happened, though the possible presence of an 'army' implies a settlement of considerable extent at the end of the first millennium.

From a mention in a thirteenth-century Lindores Abbey charter – and its prominence on the earliest-known Dundee seal – we can conclude that the young settlement of Dundee had an early parish church dedicated to St Clement, the martyred patron saint of sailors. Although its origins remain a frustrating enigma, an ancient church of that name was later recorded on the south side of High Street, where Hector Boece recalled in 1527, 'the greater part of the town's people resorted . . . where they worshipped the Saint with holy prayers'.

The presence of an early church dedicated to St Clement and his adoption as the town's titular saint is significant. Clement of Rome was Pope until AD100 when the emperor Trajan cast him into the sea tied to a stone anchor. Naturally, the Vikings had their own 'ties' to the sea and from the reign of King Alfred (871–95) Clement was medieval Denmark's most important saint. A wooden church was built in Aarhus in 1102 to contain Clement's relics and the cathedral bearing his name was begun shortly after in the Danish town. Both dates are contemporary with Scotland's earliest burgh development. We know that it was common for Scottish east-coast burghs to be formed around earlier religious institutions. We also know that the Danish conquest of parts of Britain led to the foundation of churches dedicated to Clement in urban settings by Vikings absorbed into local communities.

Researchers are still trying to determine to what extent the cult of St Clement had influence in Scotland and the importance of Danish settlement and culture on the eleventh and twelfth centuries, but non-local grey pottery fragments found in an archaeological dig in Perth High Street in 1975 – in which I was a *Time Team*-ish teenage amateur – are now thought to be Danish in origin and have been chemically dated to around 1250. Landowners around the Tay estuary had Norse personal names. Danish place names have also survived from this period. Yet we can only speculate as to the influence of visiting Scandinavians on early Dundee and whether the founding of a church dedicated to St Clement at the very heart of the old town is a sign of a Viking presence. The famous 'Oranges and Lemons' ceremony at St Clement Danes church near Fleet Street in London every March, in which the nursery rhyme is recited in honour of Danish ancestry, could be fruitfully improved by a breakfast version from a sister home of journalism . . .

> Oranges and peelers,
> Made the jam of our Keiller's.

For what it is worth, I see holy brethren living in this early Christian church, administering the heritors, tenants and townsfolk. I see them retreating to its sanctuary with their sacred relics and manuscripts in times of trouble. I see them lighting a beacon on its roof to indicate a hospitable presence to sailors and the weary traveller, and ringing a great bell at times of celebration and crisis. I see sailors, making their way to boats at the adjacent old harbour, stopping to ask the intercession of the saint who was martyred by being cast into the depths. I see St Clement's thereafter attending to the rituals that marked the passage of life – the baptisms, communions, marriages and burials of its parishioners. I see this only through a speculator's spectacles, however. Contemporary evidence is sadly lacking, or buried many metres below the seat in City Square, where this book began.

Given the armies surging to and fro, it is hardly surprising that the need for defence led to the building of a stronghold on the highest outcrop of solid rock near the shore. A castle in Dundee does not enter the historical record until 1250, but a rudimentary fort, constructed on the highest point above the shoreline – the rock on which the Episcopal Cathedral of St Paul's now stands – would have given Dundee protection and some regional importance. The naming of present-day Castle Street provides the most convenient clue to its location, and parts of the dark igneous rock on which the castle was constructed can be seen near the soaring cathedral, at the junction of Commercial Street and High Street.

It was possibly a motte and bailey castle, a structure of timber planted on a mound and protected by a defensive palisade. Its interior would typically comprise a circular timber hall or meeting place. In due time, the castle would

24

have been replaced or reinforced by a structure with thick stone curtain walls and flanking towers set at angles for defence. Thereafter the gradual infill of gaps with wooden houses formed an enclosed marketplace, now High Street, sheltered by the ramparted stronghold. A street named Flukergait, later called Nethergate, developed around other houses owned by flukers, or fishermen, whose boats rested on the riverfront behind the street. Further expansion was constrained by the physical barriers of the shore, the other hills and by areas of waterlogged ground.

Poorly positioned for landward defence, but far enough from the open sea to be safe from storms and piratical attack, the settlement expanded in the general pattern of a community spreading around a protective castle and farming the surrounding land. Footpaths led to the shore, to freshwater wells, and to the nearby Dens and Scouring Burns. The reassuring presence of a natural harbour on a navigable river offered the potential for two-way trade. The developing town's location also benefited from the visible gaps in the Sidlaws, through which hinterland merchants journeyed to buy and sell and, subject to the community's customs, contribute to its revenues.

That a thriving community existed on Dundee's present site by the year 1000 is beyond reasonable doubt, simply because the town known in subsequent years could not have begun from a standing start. In the following century it began to take on the role and significance of a mature settlement, one which functioned as an important conduit for the increasingly lucrative east-coast trading corridor, a regional market and a modest administrative centre. Dundee had emerged from its Dark Ages.

2

1000 to 1300
ON THE MAP

So the settlement that would become Dundee began to take shape just as Scotland itself was composing its boundaries and developing into an independent nation, eyed suspiciously by an acquisitive English king. This was an age when urban development was proceeding rapidly across western Europe. Towns were a medieval invention. The Romans did not build any in Scotland. The Picts did not need them. The Normans did not invade. But the eleventh and twelfth centuries brought periods of agricultural prosperity and rising population. Among the urbanised settlements that achieved burgh status at this time were Perth (c.1125), Dunfermline (c.1125), Linlithgow (c.1130), Lanark (c.1140), Forfar (1180, or earlier) and Dumfries (1180).

There is no documentary evidence of eleventh- and early twelfth-century Dundee, no contemporary narration of life and living conditions. We have to rely on Andrew de Wyntoun's late fourteenth-century chronicles of Scotland for an account of Malcolm Canmore's supposed possession of the town during his pursuit of Macbeth in 1054. From Wyntoun's history also originated speculation that a royal palace was hurriedly built in the town when King Malcolm III married the English princess Margaret Atheling in 1070. Wyntoun, prior of St

Serf's Abbey on Loch Leven, writing in the 1390s, also recorded that Malcolm's successor King Edgar fell sick and died in Dundee in 1106. This, too, is lost in the mists of history, but is suggestive of an ambulatory movement of the monarchs which would have included the growing port of Dundee. As a known administrative centre, Dundee would have benefited from visits by the peripatetic Scottish court as it moved around its kingdom to make best use of the revenues due to it.

Less open to speculation is King William the Lion's patronage of the emerging settlement in the later twelfth century. It was William (1165–1214) who put Dundee on the map before Matthew Paris – one of his acts, c.1173, referring to 'Dundeeshire', implying the existence of a regional centre. Burghal status was important in terms of privileges and trade, but if a Dundee burgh charter existed in the earlier 1100s, it was certainly missing by 1325 when Robert the Bruce was asked to reaffirm the town's 'lost' burgh liberties from earlier centuries. With no more than verbal testimony by bailies and magistrates that it had enjoyed such status as far back as the early 1100s, Robert I agreed to substantiate Dundee's ancient privileges and reconfirm its status as one of Scotland's major towns.

Historians have cited the Bruce confirmation charter of 1325 as evidence of Dundee's existence as an early Scottish burgh. This may have been wishful thinking on their part – and on the part of participating witnesses at the 1325 assembly, who would have been mindful of the benefits of trading privileges supported by royal warrant. Professor A. A. M. Duncan, who translated Robert I's charters in 1992, accepts the tradition that charters by earlier kings may have been lost in war, but states, 'The truth is that no earlier king would or could grant liberties to what was not his burgh ... and King Robert's commission makes no mention of lost charters, in contrast to the exactly parallel commission for Scone abbey.'

Duncan believes that the gathering of the great and good in Dundee on 25 June 1325 may indeed have concocted a plan to raise the town's status, but adds, 'This was surely no special gathering for this business, but a midsummer gathering of burghs for commercial reasons, to exploit the freedom of the seas won by the truce of 1325.' There appears to be no evidence of Dundee as a royal burgh before William I's reign. Certainly no reference to Dundee could be found in the 216 surviving charters and documents of David I (1124–53) that carry his authority.

What we know with certainty is that William the Lion's Dundee was established by the late twelfth century and that his brother David was really the first recorded 'Dundonian'. David, 8th Earl of Huntingdon (1152–1219), boasted unimpeachable links to Scotland's royal family. He was the younger brother of Malcolm IV and William I, successor kings of Scotland from 1153 to 1214, and a grandson of the saintly King David I. In the four years between 1178 and 1182, and presumably in return for helping his elder brother keep the peace in eastern Scotland, Earl David was granted extensive estates on both sides of the River Tay.

Earl David was an extremely powerful and influential Scottish prince. He was a friend of King Richard, Coeur de Lion (the king spoke no English), and carried one of the ceremonial swords at his coronation in 1189. The earl's estates stretched from Lincoln in the south to lands in the north-east of Scotland and included extensive areas of the Carse of Gowrie, including the royal shire of Longforgan, and parts of North Fife. Much of the earl's early life is a matter of dim and dusty doubt, but a sprinkling of early historians, including Fordon, Wyntoun and Boece, spanning the fourteenth, fifteenth and sixteenth centuries, claimed he accompanied King Richard to the Crusades, probably on his third expedition of 1187. To Boece's chronicles of 1526 is owed the romantic story of Earl David, returning from the Crusades in 1190, taking shelter at Dundee from a storm that threatened his ship with destruction. Thereby delivered from peril, he founded St Mary's church on the site of today's Old Steeple, and provided a date and a hook, 800 years on, on which to hang the city's Octocentenary celebrations of 1990.

Firmer evidence shows that Earl David married Maud, sister of the wealthy Earl of Chester, in 1190. That year he was granted by his brother William 'superiority' over Dundee and its harbour, possibly as a wedding gift. How much or how little Earl David was subsequently instrumental in the development of Dundee is difficult to ascertain. As a national figure, wider estate and court affairs would have led to his absence from his northern estates for long periods. It is clear from his charters that he conducted business in England and Scotland and kept households in both countries, run along Anglo-Norman traditions, taking an entourage of family members, advisers and servants on his travels.

It is probable, however, that his personal contribution to the town was significant. In 1190 he endowed Lindores Abbey near Newburgh – 'his most conspicuous act of piety'. He ordered a new church to be built in Dundee and dedicated it to the Virgin Mary. Later described as St

Mary's in the Fields, it usefully provides an extent or 'edge' of the town from around the late 1100s. He had authority over quarrying in Fife, pasturage on Mugdrum Island, near Newburgh, and fisheries on the Tay. He is recorded as granting a toft of land to a Robert Furmage, probably a French merchant, in Dundee, and it can be gleaned from his chartulary, entrusted to trained scribes, that he imposed a constable on the town.

Above all, Dundee was commercially important to Earl David. Through his intervention valuable trading concessions were secured. In 1199 he obtained exemption for Dundee ships from harbour dues across Britain, with the exception of London. He is likely to have made improvements to the harbour to allow his town's fleet to expand to take advantage of this favourable arrangement, and to launch trading links with the coast and the Continent. With an eye landward, he would have re-fortified the castle to defend burgh privileges, almost certainly replacing any remaining timber framework with stone. Thus, under Earl David's merchant adventurism, the new burgh prospered, attracting traders from its rich agricultural hinterland to congregate at its markets and put down roots. His powerful patronage set Dundee on the way to becoming a medieval administrative and mercantile centre of considerable influence.

Earl David survived into the next century, dying in June 1219, but not before he had told the educated world – in Latin script, in a charter to Arbroath Abbey – that Dundee was *meo burgi de Dundie*, 'my burgh'. He left the town to his thirteen-year-old son and heir, John, and in fine fettle: during this period of economic stability it grew in population, built new houses in stone long before other towns and expanded its harbour. The Golden Age of peace and prosperity in the reign of Alexander III (1249–86) continued and enhanced the feeling of well-being.

It is thus easier to understand why the thirteenth-century monk and medieval chronicler Matthew Paris included Dundee so prominently when he began his map of Great Britain at St Albans Abbey around 1240. The Paris map in the British Library was the first to attempt to portray the physical appearance of the whole country. It shows the boundary between Scotland and England marked by Hadrian's Wall. Further north is the Antonine Wall, built by Hadrian's successor. The gaping mouths of the Forth and Tay are clearly marked, with Edinburgh and Dundee in their true positions some 300 years before exact surveying was allowed by the invention of triangulation. Paris can be forgiven for the veering, eastwards slant of the Scottish mainland, since, politically and economically, much has gravitated westwards and to the central belt in centuries since.

The journalist in me wonders how Paris knew what he was mapping. Was he pot-shotting at how Britain looked and included Dundee because he had eavesdropped on a business conversation that mentioned the growing town, its castle, its markets and fairs, its accommodating harbour and its first guildry of merchants, formed around that time? Or is his projection, although askew at points, evidence of what actually existed in the neglected Dark Ages of Dundee's history? Does his inclusion of the port among only a handful of correct Scottish references suggest its regional importance in the early 1200s?

To an extent we can be confident of Paris's social status and learning. He was on chummy terms with Henry III and visited his court in London. His work drew on information from the brethren monks, travellers and traders who stopped for the night at St Albans, on the main road north from the capital. There is evidence, too, that he copied compass points from the second-century Alexandrian geographer Ptolemy's recording of landmarks around the British coast. Paris's literary credentials also seem beyond reproach. He was respected in his own lifetime for his historical knowledge, for which the monks of St Albans had long been famous. His *Chronica Major*, which told of world events until the year of his death in 1259, is considered among the most important historical writing of the thirteenth century.

Sure, Paris's map is askew in many respects. Arbroath is in Sutherland, Dumbarton somewhere in the western Highlands and the Orkneys keep Dundee company in the Firth of Tay. Glasgow is near Edinburgh, and Brechin occupies the position of Perth. But Dundee is in its proper geographical location, and probably for good reason. We know that Dundee's harbour was active at that time. By 1212, its merchants were trading with London markets. In 1225, Alexander II granted to the abbot of Coupar Angus Abbey a licence for its vessels to export goods to Flanders, while French wine was imported no later than 1262 for forwarding to Forfar. Although Paris may not have visited Scotland, he may easily have met someone with knowledge of Scotland's dominant east-coast ports – and local drinking habits.

It is just as well that Matthew Paris was diligent. By the end of the thirteenth century Edward I was trying to wipe the town off the map.

At the core of the cross-border conflict was the disputed succession to the crown. Scotland's royal line had been extinguished on the unexpected death of the infant queen Margaret, Maid of Norway, in 1290. At least a dozen men put their names, or swords, forward for the job of king. John de Balliol and Robert de Brus, grandfather of Robert the Bruce, supported by powerful factions, emerged as principal claimants. Both agreed to refer the decision to the arbitration of the veteran Edward I of England. Edward met the Scottish nobility and clergy in 1291 and persuaded the more pliable Balliol to place Scotland under English feudal control in return for possession of the crown.

Edward declared for Balliol in November 1292, prefacing his declaration with another in which he assumed for himself the superiority of Scotland. Edward's armies, handily massed on the border, poured into Scotland to take possession of his new fiefdom. In an order to Dundee that month, Edward declared Balliol King of Scotland and demanded the town's castle 'together with everything else' be delivered to his garrison. The castle appears to have been ceded without bloodshed. But when, in 1295, Edward learned that his mock king had quietly rekindled Scotland's auld alliance with France and had undermined, then renounced, England's authority over Scotland, he marched with a great army towards Edinburgh and put the Scots to the sword at Dunbar. Edward reached Dundee in June 1296, on his great warhorse Bayard, purloining the Stone of Scone along the way, and met with little resistance. He continued north to Brechin where he stripped the humiliated Balliol of the crown and sent him south to the Tower as Balliol's supporters scattered to the four winds and disowned involvement. On his southward journey, Edward destroyed Dundee's new church, imposed an intimidating, combative garrison in its castle, and set back a century of development.

It is at this point that the future patriot and warlord

William Wallace, apocryphally a former scholar at Dundee's school, intervened by gathering an army and beginning his life's mission to resist English occupation. We are indebted to the chronicler Blind Harry the minstrel (c.1440–92) for the slender Wallace link to Dundee. In his historical but largely fanciful narrative *Ye Actis and Deidis of ye Illuster and Vailzeand Campioun Schir Wilham Wallace*, composed 200 years after the events, Harry commented that, 'Upon a day to Dunde he [Wallace] was send.' During this visit to the town in which Blind Harry says he was schooled, Wallace confronted the son of the English governor Selbie near Dundee Castle and attacked him in an underhand manner:

> Fast by the collar Wallace couth hym ta,
> Undyr hys hand ye knyff he bradit owt,
> For all hys men yat semblyt hym about,
> Bot help himself, he wist of no remede,
> Without reskew he stykit him to dede,
> Ye squire fell – of hym yar was na mar.

Wallace (1270–1305) may or may not have been educated in Dundee, which had established its first school in 1239 when the abbots of Lindores were granted a charter to 'plant schools wherever they please in the burgh'. More likely, he was schooled in the Paisley area or in Ayrshire. Nonetheless, Dundee was heavily involved in the Wars of Independence and with the freedom fighter who was adopted as Guardian of Scotland. It was Wallace, by tradition, who galvanised the Scottish clans to act where the nobility would not and retake the strongholds occupied by the English. One of his first Acts, signed at Torphichen in March 1298, was to elevate to the hereditary title of Constable of Dundee his lieutenant Alexander Scrymgeour, awarding him, 'Six marks of land in the territory of Dundee . . . and also the constabulary of the castle of Dundee . . . for faithful service and carrying the royal banner in the army of Scotland.'

A stained-glass window in today's City Chambers depicts Wallace directing the 1297 siege against the garrison at Dundee alongside Alexander 'Schyrmeschur'. Wallace, in fact, left the town to its own fate under Scrymgeour while he fought the invading English army at Stirling Bridge. Dundee was always better at trading than fighting in any case. While Wallace was engaging the English at Stirling, leaving 5000 dead on the field, Dundee's merchants were entertaining traders from the Continental port of Lubeck where, coincidentally, the only genuine document bearing Wallace's signature is held.

Internecine problems, plot and counter-plot, were seldom distant in developing Dundee. By the end of the thirteenth century, the town was governed locally by two bodies: its municipal council – formed by the most trustworthy inhabitants, all male naturally – and the rival office of constable of the castle, the kingly appointment restored by Wallace. Imagine yourself on a summer's day in 1298, walking steeply downhill from the house fortified by Scrymgeour at Dudhope to the council tollbooth near City Square, and it is not difficult to visualise the open marshland separating the two oligarchies in medieval Dundee, each eyeing the other suspiciously, anxious of any power-broking moves. The townsfolk appointed its council and generally detested the king's choice of constable, and no doubt the ill feeling was reciprocated. It was astute diplomacy by the Franciscans in 1289 to establish their Greyfriars seminary between the two – or perhaps the brethren of the ancient order wanted their daily bread buttered on both sides, or to have their Dundee cake and eat it.

One reason we do not know much of what went on in this early period of Dundee's history is the absence of official documents. Edward I not only hammered the Scots, but is generally believed to have removed or destroyed records which would have shone a light on the town's earlier history. As George Buchanan, the trustworthy chronicler, noted wistfully in 1582, 'Not content with having removed all those who appeared likely to produce any revolution, Edward bent his soul, if possible, to abolish the very name of the nation . . . he destroyed every history, treaty and ancient monument, whether left by the Romans or erected by the Scots, and carried off all the books and teachers of learning into England.' Alexander Scrymgeour was also carried off by Edward – and hanged at Newcastle.

New evidence has emerged about the ordinary people who followed in the footsteps of Dundee's earliest settlers as the thirteenth century drew to a close – enough to reconstruct a picture of their lifestyle and living conditions. In 1992, workmen at the City Churches in Nethergate unearthed a number of bones and skeletons. As usual, it was assumed they were the remains of soldiers or civilians slaughtered in the Cromwellian crackdown of 1651, when General Monk's army sacked the town. Instead, the Scottish Urban Archaeological Trust (now SUAT) showed that the finds came from an undocumented medieval cemetery of an earlier, or even the original, St Mary's church, as they were underneath and thus predated the Steeple of the mid-1400s. The presence of this medieval graveyard, with bodies buried in 'conventional, individual graves', significantly helps to confirm the burgh's early history. It also debunks knee-jerk conclusions that burials around the Steeple are necessarily Monk's doing.

In 1993, a Ninewells-based consultant rheumatologist, a consultant radiologist and a junior house physician with an interest in archaeology, joined SUAT archaeologists to conduct a detailed examination of the bones. Together they analysed the skeletal remains of around seventy people presumed to have died in the twelfth or thirteenth centuries, up to 500 years before Monk's massacre. Bones were radiographed and dental remains examined at Dundee Dental Hospital. The researchers were surprised to discover that most of the remains came from strong, fit, youngish people who were sufficiently well nourished to achieve their full growth potential. The team believed the bones were from 'an artisan group whose lives were probably used to hard physical labour' – day-to-day lifting, pulling, pushing and walking. The doctors calculated the heights of adult medieval Dundonians to 5ft 6in for males and 5ft 2in for females and concluded, 'The general conception seems to be that Dundonians were and are shorter than the average members of the Scottish population. Our results, however, suggest that the height of medieval citizens was similar to their modern-day counterparts and not significantly different from the national population.'

This was not the position when Dundee Social Union found in 1904 that the city's working-class children were 'under the standard' in respect of height and weight, and were smaller and lighter when compared with Harris Academy pupils from the affluent West End.

Over ninety per cent of the medieval group died before

the age of forty-six, the typical lifespan for the period. The fact that the men appeared to have lived longer than the women was attributed to death through pregnancy and childbirth. Teeth were ground down but showed little decay, implying a diet mainly of coarse stoneground meal and very little sugar . . . in other words, teeth in twelfth-century Dundee were better than those in our mouths in the twenty-first. Also surprising was the lack of evidence of nutritional disease in the bones. The researchers concluded that the fertile nature of the area had played a role in sustaining robust health. There was no evidence of leprosy or tuberculosis, and a low rate of osteoarthritis. These Dundonians were as healthy as they could be.

Non-aristocratic inhabitants of medieval Dundee would have lived in functional timber dwellings. Roofs were probably thatched with straw or Tay reeds. Interiors usually included a basic table and stools made from oak or elm, turned wood food vessels, iron or bone utensils and pottery cooking dishes either imported or made at a kiln located far enough from housing not to be a fire hazard. Light was provided by oil-filled lamps and candles. Deposits discovered by earlier archaeologists indicate diets rich in beef, pork, deer, wild birds and chicken. Dairy produce, such as eggs, and vegetables were part of every-day domestic production. Cereals, particularly oats and barley, were a dietary mainstay and Dundee diets in particular were rich in salmon. The backlands to the street frontages – the long strips of land which passed down to us as urban plot sizes – were used for trades such as leather-making, blacksmithing, the stabling of horses and the storage of agricultural implements. Tools were made of iron with wooden handles, in the way they were made in Roman times, in the way that some are made today.

This tantalising glimpse of Dundee in its earliest burghal form paints a compelling canvas of a thriving, healthy community; where work involved the ancient skills of farming, hunting and fishing; where religion also played a great part in local life, with friars and priests an everyday sight, and where hardy adventurers established the first trading links with the coastal regions and the Continent to export wool and hides. Remarkably, our idea that violence was an everyday occurrence in the Dark Ages is not supported by these reconstructed fragments from our past. Archaeologists reported in 2000 that injuries to the people who lived in medieval Dundee were caused by 'accident rather than as a result of inter-personal violence'. The most traumatic injury noted was a broken arm.

It seems we could have learned much from these happy, healthy Dundonians, whose ancient bones were carefully re-interred in the Eastern Necropolis after a short service.

3

1300 TO 1500
SCOTLAND'S BIRTHPLACE

Angus, the SNP-controlled county neighbouring Dundee, raised eyebrows in 2005 by marketing itself on welcoming signs and its website as 'Scotland's Birthplace'. It based this colourful nonsense on the signing of the Declaration of Independence at Arbroath Abbey in 1320 and the one-time presence of the Pictish 'capital' near Forfar. One could, of course, stake a claim for another neighbour in this respect. Perth was the crowning place of Scottish kings and once capital of Scotland. Let us position ourselves instead on the historical edge by nominating Dundee for the title.

The Wars of Independence threw the kingly spotlight on two principals – John Balliol, the legitimate Scottish king according to Edward I of England and, after Balliol's expulsion, the people's choice in Scotland, the iconic Robert the Bruce. Both claimants to the throne were lineal descendants of Earl David, who had put Dundee on the map a century earlier. Balliol was his great-grandson through a marriage to Earl David's eldest daughter. Bruce was his great-great grandson through a marriage to his second daughter. As noted, Earl David's link to the royal line was undisputed: he was the grandson of the brilliant King David I and younger brother of Malcolm IV and William I – the Lion. Importantly, when the royal line of

William I expired in 1290, David's descendants became the legitimate candidates for the throne.

John Balliol's ultimately successful claim was based on the fact that his mother Devorguilla was the daughter of Margaret, eldest daughter of Earl David. In effect, he was Earl David's heir – or, as *Debrett's Peerage* might put it, he pleaded primogeniture in legitimate, cognatic line. But Robert de Brus, grandfather to the eventual King Robert the Bruce, also believed he had a right to the throne through a more manly descent from Earl David's second daughter, Isabella.

Earl David also had three sons by his wife Maud of Chester, and it was to his teenage son and heir, John, that 'ownership' of Dundee passed on the earl's death in 1219, John's elder brothers Henry and David having not lived long enough to inherit. When John died, the lands in and around Dundee passed to Earl David's two eldest surviving daughters: Margaret – who was married in Dundee in 1206 – and Isabella. Two illegitimate sons, both called Henry, inherited lands at Longforgan and Brechin, while a third daughter, Ada, received an estate at Newtyle.

The legacy of Margaret's daughter Devorguilla, the favourite of Earl David and mother of the ill-starred John Balliol, included lands in central Dundee, where she also founded the Franciscan monastery on the site of the Howff, c.1289, perhaps near to her mother's house. She had previously paid for the foundation of Balliol College at Oxford in 1282. Her lands in Dundee were probably bequeathed to her son John Balliol after her death in 1290. They may in any case have fallen to him when he was made king by Edward I two years later. Meanwhile Margaret's sister Isabella bequeathed lands at Hilltown and Milton of Craigie in Dundee to the Abbey of Lindores.

Thus it is entirely probable that much of Dundee fell under the superiority of the Bruce and Balliol families as the kingship of Scotland was decided, and became what it would become in the linen and jute era of the 1800s – a women's town. Add the potent symbol of nationhood when Wallace 'struck the first blow for independence' in Dundee, and it does not seem so naïve to regard Dundee as fundamental to Scotland's story.

Yet the fourteenth century had hardly begun before the English returned in 1303, led by Edward, the white-haired king who would soon have *Scottorum Malleus* ('Hammer of the Scots') engraved on his tombstone. Edward's army destroyed the parts of the castle left standing from the previous attack. In the revolt-crushing offensive that followed, Wallace was captured, hanged, drawn and quartered in 1305 – and if he was a former pupil of the town, he is probably the only FP to have had his head lopped off and his severed legs sent on tour around Scotland. Bruce, crowned king at Scone in 1306, endured several military reverses, not least a rout at Methven Wood while he was offering protection to foreign merchants landed at Dundee.

Edward II, who succeeded his father as king of England in the summer of 1307, had Dundee Castle rebuilt and garrisoned. The new king wrote to his 'beloved and faithful subjects' in Dundee in 1309 encouraging them to hold out against the 'rebel' Scots until reinforcements arrived. A record survives of orders to forward supplies of corn, malt, beans and wine to eight garrisons in Scotland, of which Dundee's was probably the hungriest. The town's strategic importance to the English cannot be in doubt, given the priority accorded to securing its castle.

By early 1311, forces loyal to Bruce led by his fiery

brother Edward were laying siege to the castle. From the safety of York, Edward II issued an order to his 'beloved and faithful' subjects not to surrender 'our town of Dundee', adding cheerfully, 'on pain of death and dismemberment'. Another hurried despatch from York in February 1311 praised the resilience of the castle governor William de Montefitchet: 'You have manfully laboured in the midst of dangers, and been loyal to the cause.' The king gave thanks that the garrison had 're-pulsed attacks on our said town' and entreated the governor to continue the spirited defence. As the siege dragged on, the headstrong, capricious Edward issued a peremptory order to the influential strongholds of Berwick and Newcastle instructing the ports to send men, supplies, ammunition and 'as much cash as you can spare' by sea to 'our said beleaguered town' of Dundee. The anxious demand for money implies the 130 knights and horsemen accommodated at the castle were unpaid and unhappy. With the garrison's provisions increasingly depleted, the tone of Edward's messages became urgent and threatening. From York in March 1311: 'We command you, under forfeiture of life and members, and every other penalty in our power to inflict, that you will not give up the custody of our town of Dundee.'

All the king's horses and all the king's men could not save the situation. Early in 1312, the castle was ceded by negotiation, leaving the English garrison at Perth cut off from the sea. Bruce probably had it demolished, as was his habit, to prevent it being used in the event of any reversal of fortune. He had done so in 1308 at nearby Forfar Castle, which was at the time 'stuffit all with yngliss men'. There is also a possibility that his fiery brother Edward, known for his short fuse, blew up Dundee Castle to prevent it falling again to the enemy, and to allow the Scots forces to concentrate elsewhere. Torrie (1990) confirms the stronghold's absence from records after the Battle of Bannockburn in 1314, though, of course, its legacy is today's Castle Street and arty signage for Castlehill.

Robert the Bruce retired with his court to Dundee shortly after his great victory in 1314, adding to our developing picture of Dundee as the nation's birthplace. It was in Dundee that a national council of the Scottish clergy – the nation's leading bishops and abbots – declared him to be the lawful king of Scotland. This gathering took place in the Greyfriars monastery, a building founded by the rival Balliol family. In 1325 Robert I also left a legacy to the town by issuing a charter delineating a plot of ground for a tollbooth. This charter authorised an area eighty feet long by forty feet broad for the town's new council chamber and prison. Eighteenth-, nineteenth- and twentieth-century histories of Dundee took this to mean a location in the Seagate, their original heart of the town. This view percolated down to accounts as recent as Ferguson (2005), who concluded that it was 'probably where Peter Street meets the Seagate today'. E. P. D. Torrie, in the best study of medieval Dundee, also located the land grant in Seagate: 'Seagait remained the commercial nucleus of the town until the fourteenth century, which is confirmed by the grant of land by Robert I in 1325 for the erection of a Tollbooth there.'

After re-examining the 1325 charter, A. A. M. Duncan reported to me that, 'The Seagait market is a complete ghost, and with it we must disregard the Seagait as the original nucleus of the burgh away back in 1190.' This idea was based, he said, on an erroneous reading of Robert I's charter of 1325. Instead, Duncan suggested that

Seagate was too narrow a street for a marketplace, and that the tollbooth was always on a site near today's City Square, where it acted over the centuries as the burgh's court, its prison and the building where market dues and tolls were collected and counted.

The mention of the tidal waters of the Tay reaching the south side of Seagate in a charter as late as 1414 supports Duncan's re-interpretation of the burgh's early documentary evidence. This implies that part of the Seagate was very close to the shore some 300 years after the burgh's beginnings, and that it was still affected by high tides. Indeed, the bookseller William Kidd recalled as recently as 1896 the river flowing up to the houses at the back of Seagate. Given this exposure to the sea it is an unconvincing location for the burgh's early settlement.

In his study of the town's archaeology David Perry (2005) suggested that, in fact, the Seagate may have begun as nothing more grand than 'a back lane to the rear of the properties on Murraygate, before being developed into a street in its own right'. Rather, burials, pottery and timbers from the excavations along the line from the Old Steeple to today's Wellgate Centre place the principal burgh buildings of King Robert's time firmly to the west of Castlehill.

There was also a natural inclination to erect a cross, essentially as a symbol of Christian faith, but in practice a place for burgesses to buy and sell, hence the adoption of the name Market Cross. We do not know what the first Dundee cross looked like, but it is recorded in the marketplace in 1442. Its original site was also probably in the City Square area close to where Desperate Dan patrols, despite the commemorative cross of stones marking its supposed spot at the intersection of Peter Street and Seagate.

Although only fragmentary evidence remains, the pre-eminence of a marketplace in a central location is further emphasised by the creation there around 1360 of the tron, the public weigh beam on which the price of goods was determined. This was located at a site in front of the main entrance to the Overgate centre. The concentration of markets and business near St Clement's and St Mary's in this west end of today's High Street subsequently encouraged new building in the Flukergait (Nethergate) and Argyllgait (Overgate), nudging the burgh boundaries in a north-westerly direction, away from the river.

Robert I continued his association with the evolving town, aiding its growth by granting a charter in 1328, allowing its burgesses a trading monopoly over the sheriffdom of Forfar. Customs accounts for 1326–7 show eighteen ships sailing from the harbour with cargoes of wool, hides and sheepskins. Within five years, the number of vessels had risen to twenty-eight, implying strong growth of the medieval port. As usual, Dundee merchants held swords in one hand while signing contracts with the other. As the Wars of Independence continued into the 1330s, Dundee was exporting an average of 120 tonnes of wool annually to the Continent. By the 1340s the word 'shipmaster' was appearing in local documents, the town possessed a 'great trade of merchandise' and was listed as one of the four 'Great Towns' in Scotland by the leading port of Bruges. By the 1370s, Dundee was contributing over ten per cent of Scotland's customs dues.

Published histories of Dundee relate how the fourteenth century was not allowed to pass without Dundee being trashed again. John of Gaunt, uncle of the mischievous Richard II – who had learned his trade fighting with his brother Edward, the Black Prince in the Hundred

Years' War – is said to have led the marauding English to attack Dundee in 1385. This account is attributable to the French historian Jean Froissart (1337–1405), who recorded that, 'The English burned Dundee and spared neither monasteries nor churches, but put all to fire and sword.' It is probable, however, that Froissart mistook Dundee for Dunbar.

One can imagine a collective sigh of relief as the 1400s came along. For once there was no invasion to kick off a new century. Instead the plague returned, moving from house to house, then street to street. A council record for 1403 lists Robert de Guthry as the only bailie present at a council meeting, as 'the other bailies had died of plague'. One can imagine the shrieking distress of the bereaved as 'death lorded over all'. One is also left to wonder how many citizens took to ships to escape the disease-ridden town. The harbour in the early 1400s remained in its original position, a natural haven, free from silting, at the southern end of today's Crichton Street. By the early fifteenth century it probably comprised a solidly-built breakwater pier made from timber cages reinforced with piled stones and boulders. From there vessels plied lucrative coastal and foreign routes. And yet the first documented reference to a built harbour at Dundee is in 1447, when James II passed legislation authorising dues to be levied on vessels to provide revenues for its repair. As trade increased, one entry in the burgh court books instructed skippers to tie up vessels tidily by the bulwarks to avoid obstructing other traffic. Those who moored carelessly faced a fine of £10 Scots – enough to burn a hole in any merchant's pocket.

Flemish weavers had settled in or near Dundee by the early 1400s. The Flemings taught local people to weave and their cloth was exported from Dundee by 1434. The rough cloth was known as 'plaiding'. It was dyed in different colours and used by the armies of the Low Countries and the Baltic. It was also the cloth normally worn by local men below their Hilltown bonnets, and women wore plaid shrouds in public. Customs records show the continued growth of the port, sending out in 1479, '205 score and 6 doz ells of woollen cloth'. In 1497 seven Dundee vessels entered Baltic ports, the largest number from any Scottish burgh.

St Mary's Tower and the town centre's west-east alignment provide the only tangible reminders of this once thriving Middle Ages community. What we see today as we look at the elderly Steeple is more or less what its builders intended in the mid-1400s when it replaced an earlier church. We do not know for certain when it was begun and completed, but it probably falls between an agreement with Lindores Abbey to build a new choir in 1442 and the gift of 'ane gryt bell' to St Mary's in 1495.

The unique, telescopic Steeple, rising in five stages to its abutments at 156 feet, is now the highest surviving ecclesiastical medieval tower in Scotland. Inside, many altars were endowed by the abbots of Lindores out of taxes and donations squeezed from the burgh. An inventory of its ornaments in 1454 included, 'twa missals, a chalice of silver with ane crystal stane in the midst'. By the end of the 1400s St Mary's bell would have replaced beacons on the Law as the town's harbinger of celebration and danger. And by then the town's ships were passing under the protective guns of Broughty Castle, completed as a great fortress in 1496. This was not the drawbridged tourist attraction which invites visitors to three floors of exhibits today. This romanticised replica, a

Victorian notion of medievalism, was constructed around the original core of the castle in 1861, complete with 'contemporary' musket-ball holes peppering its masonry.

Both the auld enemy and the auld alliance must have been talking points as the century ended. In 1489, Sir Andrew Wood of Largo, leading two ships of the Royal Scottish Navy, defeated three English privateers in the mouth of the Tay as inhabitants crowded to the shore to cheer on their countrymen during the exchange. Wood brought them as prizes into Dundee where the dead were buried and the wounded treated at a new hospital in the Nethergate. Stephen Bull, the notorious English commander, was taken by Wood to Edinburgh and presented to James IV. Instead of resorting to the customary bargaining and demands, the chivalrous king praised the gallantry of Bull and his crews and without exacting any ransom sent them home with their ships as a gift to the English king. The unwritten message, presumably, was that they would not be so well entertained the next time.

The following year, a company of French comedians set up their booth on the public playfield at West Port, entertaining crowds with pre-Reformation ribaldry, which probably lightened the mood at the end of the traumatic 1400s, while setting the scene for the Wedderburns' incendiary anti-Catholic plays of the following century. Their audience, seated on the grassy banks near Witches Knowe in West Port, watching players, musicians and jesters on hastily-constructed platforms, were the beginnings of a theatrical tradition continued brilliantly today at Dundee Rep.

War and peace. It sums up the story of Dundee's first 400 years as a burgh. And when James IV rounded off the century with a visit to Dundee in 1492, he found a community acting as a collection and distribution point for an extensive hinterland and ideally positioned to benefit from North Sea trade. Yet Dundee's vulnerable location on the exposed shoreline always left it open to attack. Driving along Dock Street to Broughty Ferry, we can imagine when its castle was still a formidable fortress, and reflect on those looking instinctively for approaching trouble on the estuary as they passed along the same thoroughfare 500 years ago.

4

1500 TO 1700
GROWING PAINS

At the start of the sixteenth century, the town looked like this. There was a small but bustling harbour approximately on the site of Tayside House. A network of narrow wynds and vennels led to the Marketgate (the present High Street/Murraygate) and the Flukergait (later Nethergate). Beyond the marketplace was the emerging Argyllgait (later Overgate). Thorter Row now ran through blocks of houses between the Marketgate and Overgate. Beyond the Overgate port to the north lay the town's common ground and playfields. South of the centre, streets had been rescued from the river. Seagate followed the line of the shore to the pastureland beyond Cowgate. St Mary's rose majestically above all of this and dominated the skyline.

There were two churches, a monastery, and the town was on the cusp of building its second friary for the Dominicans. Burials took place in the Howff, where there was now a charge for interments – twelve pence for a man, less for a child's grave and free for 'poor creaturis'. Buying and selling of merchandise, proclamations and gossip took place at the Mercat Cross, around which were placed instruments of punishment, including pillory, jougs and cuckold stool. Luckenbooths faced the market square and municipal business was conducted at the tollbooth. The town's leper house was safely beyond the city boundaries at Blackscroft, and its inhabitants securely separated among 'lodges' set aside for those stricken with plague. The Hilltown, a rival barony, was divided from the town by a footpath. Its youths 'perturbs the burgh mony ways, the maist part of them nocht native, but coming furth of the Hill'. Any caught, warned the burgesses, 'shall be banishit for ever'.

Charles McKean is Professor of Scottish architectural history at Dundee University and the historian who has done most to dispel the notion of Dundee as an also-ran before the advent of jute. Once he showed me a little-known lane behind Crichton Street which he called The-One-Behind-Crichton-Street. 'Look,' he said. 'We're surrounded by medieval buildings. Crichton Street is 1772. This' [he points] 'is probably 1552. The close is curving to keep the wind out of the marketplace and would have gone down to the sea.'

Then the leading architectural academic is off to the little-known Scott's Close, south of Nethergate, which is also on his restoration wish list – a hidden jumble of medieval buildings, courtyards and gardens. 'We are standing,' he says in hushed tones, 'on another of the ancient routes from the harbour to the town's parish church.'

McKean's point is that parts of Dundee in the 1500s and 1600s – the largely undocumented period of development between the housing of the Middle Ages and the grander stone structures of the eighteenth century – is not a mythical entity, but a physical presence, waiting to be discovered behind today's Victorian and twentieth-century façades. McKean co-wrote a ground-breaking architectural guide to Dundee in 1984. He was told by scoffing peers in Edinburgh that it would make a 'pamphlet'. Its 1993 reprint had close to 200 pages. Since then he has shattered perceptions by showing how Dundee competed with Aberdeen for the status as Scotland's second city for 400 years, and how the town's renaissance of cultural learning and social life recovered its spirit from the medieval preoccupation with death and the soul.

McKean's views are supported by ongoing work at Gardyne's Land, located behind 71 High Street, a group of three linked buildings newly restored to provide youth hostel accommodation. Tree ring dating of its oak timbers suggests a date of construction around 1600, but a sequence of layers of imported pottery dating from the twelfth to the fourteenth centuries hints at occupancy by wealthy families at the earliest period of the burgh and confirms early mercantile settlement in the High Street area. The surviving four-storey and double-attic merchant's house, resplendent with sumptuous decoration, would have been pointed out proudly to visitors as indicative of Dundee's ambitious forward thinking. It is, indeed, a rare survivor in McKean's medieval masterclass.

Dundee and Aberdeen were linked in the early 1500s by Hector Boece, a native and resident of Dundee and later first principal of Aberdeen University. Boece's claim to fame outside Aberdeen rests on his *Scotorum Historiae*, a flowery history of Scotland published in 1526 in Paris, where he had been sent to study after the Wars of Independence threw Scotland into the arms of France. *Scotorum Historiae*, now the oldest printed book in his home town's library, is frequently criticised as medieval imagination at work and dismissed as fallacious and unworthy of serious scrutiny. In fact, it was only Scotland's second published history and was the first to be written in a readable style. In a remarkable cycle of copying which anticipated today's internet plagiarists, Boece's work was circulated widely, won royal approval, and was translated from Latin into flowing Scots by John Bellenden in 1536, apparently because James V's Latin was lacking. Bellenden's text is regarded today as the first Scottish book of vernacular prose. Later translated into English for Raphael Holinshed's *Chronicles*, Bellenden's account of Boece's narrative was also used by Shakespeare as the basis for Macbeth.

Boece (c.1465–1536) must have formed a formidable intellect during his impressionable years in Dundee. He was a professor of divinity, medicine and philosophy in France and Scotland, and formed a lasting friendship with the great arbiter of learning Erasmus, who not only swayed Europe with his writing, but also twice put pen to paper in Boece's praise. By the time of his death, Boece's reputation was established across Europe. Admittedly his *Scotorum Historiae* is at times a work of patriotic and occasionally audacious fiction. It is also generously sprinkled with good-natured myths – among them his claim that in his day the dried bones of English soldiers lay in the streets with labels narrating the manner of their death attached to their lifeless limbs. He was not the last historian to add arms and legs to create a local myth, though. And it was not all tittle-tattle and invention. Dundee was, for example, 'the town quhair we were born' and where 'mony virtewus and lauborius pepill are in making of claith'.

Boece had passed away peacefully by the time plague arrived in his home town in 1544, sending many Dundonians to an early grave. George Wishart, one of his contemporaries, was in that year a Protestant preacher exhorting anti-Catholicism in Dundee and elsewhere. At Cambridge, where he previously taught, Wishart was described by his friend Emery Tylney as follows: 'A man of tall stature . . . blacke haired, long-bearded, comely of personage, well-spoken of after his countrey of Scotland, courteous, lowly [lovely], glad to teach, desirous to learn, and was well travelled, having on him, for his habit or clothing, nothing but a mantel or frize gown to the shoes, a blacke Millian dublet, and plain blacke hosen; coarse new canvasse for his shirtes, and white falling bandes and cuffes at the hands. All the which apparel he gave to the poor, some weekly, some monethly, some quarterlie, as he liked, save his French cap, which he kept the whole yeare of my being with him.'

On hearing that plague had spread to Dundee, the self-denying Wishart travelled to the town and preached to the infected gathered beyond the city's gates. He was regarded as a miracle-worker by the inhabitants, not because of his bravery or foolhardiness in disregarding his own safety, but because he had apparent immunity from the disease that killed so many. A greater miracle is that the stone arch in Cowgate, from which Wishart is said to have preached, materialised long after his death. Recent archaeological trenching nearby discovered the medieval street level nearly three feet below the present road surface, raising the possibility of ancient foundations at other sites in the city.

Wishart had united the reformists of the medieval church in Scotland with proselytising zeal. For doing so, he was hunted down by Cardinal Beaton, the genuflecting, sacrament-absorbed Catholic primate of Scotland. Beaton, who belonged to the off-with-their-ears cruel school, sent an assassin to Dundee to take care of the hated Protestant preacher, but the hireling was chased from the town. Another attempt to kill Wishart near Montrose also failed. Wishart was said to have faced a third attempt on his life in Dundee before hiring a giant minder to walk before him with a discouraging two-handed sword – a duty conferred at one point on his young disciple John Knox. But in March 1546, he was cornered by Beaton's men, arrested, charged with heresy and sentenced to death by burning in front of the Episcopal palace, while Beaton callously watched from a window. Three months later, religious reformers stormed the palace and in revenge for Wishart's death threw Beaton out of the same window before putting him to death.

The stirring of Protestant feeling and the coming of the Reformation in 1560 resonated with a rapidly-converting town which had stealthily imported Tyndall's bible from England and filled its returning ships from Danzig with Lutheran tracts. As early as 1521, and before a string of Protestant martyrs were burned, several Dundee women were convicted of heresy and banished. The first iconoclastic attacks on buildings in Scotland took place in Dundee in 1543 when its monasteries were desecrated. A contemporary journal of events noted, 'Thair was ane great heresie in Dundie; thair they destroyt the kirkis.' The interior of St Clement's, also a casualty, was ripped out and the building eventually made way for a weigh house in 1560 and a new tollbooth on the south side of High Street in 1562. Stones from Greyfriars were used for a flesh market or slaughterhouse further along the High Street, close to today's dragon sculpture. And of medieval St Mary's only its stoutly built west tower survived the Reformation, its historic Steeple.

The destruction of buildings which had added an important spiritual dimension to people's lives was probably unpopular with many, though it is likely that the Reformation was generally welcomed in a town that revered the Protestant martyr Wishart, which had strong trading links with the Lutheran Low Countries and which hosted several general assemblies of the Church of Scotland following the disruption. The valuable church lands passed to the town council at this time which, along with the useful income they provided would, no doubt, have smoothed misgivings and any sense of loss.

With the unpredictable Henry VIII 'burning Protestant and Catholic alike, on the same day, and in the same fire,' in George Buchanan's account, fortifications were deemed necessary on Dundee's unprotected landward side. The ports or gateways – Cowgate, Seagate, Wellgate, Murraygate, Overgate, Nethergate and West Port – already served as collection points for tolls and taxes, but gained a wider remit to control entry and exit. But the town's poor defensive embankments could not keep out pneumonic plague and they could not hold back its enemies. Overlooked from the north and open to the sea, Dundee was as defenceless a location as one could imagine. Sure enough, in 1547 Henry VIII's battle fleet sailed unmolested up the Tay, garrisoned Broughty Castle and destroyed much of Dundee by naval bombardment. In the estuarial stronghold the English remained, besieged by Scots and their Continental allies, and doubtless proving an intimidating nuisance to shipping trade. In January 1548, the English emerged from the castle to attempt to take the town, before burning the Steeple, pinching its bells and withdrawing. In December that year, another attack on the town was launched. That foray, too, was abandoned, but the English destroyed St Mary's, burned lesser churches and convents, the tollbooth, school and almshouses during their retreat. The town's first clock, installed in the Steeple only in 1546, was dismantled and taken as war booty to England.

The community took a long time to recover from the hostile assault of the garrison, which was finally forced out by French troops in 1550. Jean de Beague, one of the French soldiers, noted his 'mortification to find nobody in it but some poor women and a few men who were labouring hard to extinguish the flames the English had kindled'. Such was the destruction that, in 1556, a ban was placed on the export of Sidlaw slates – 3900 had been sent for St Giles church in Edinburgh the previous year – because of the need to repair damage caused by the attacks. Torrie (1990) recorded that the town's sorry situation helped it to win a sympathetic remission from taxes for the next thirty years, and that, 'The burgh records as late as 1582 speak of property lying "wastit and brunt".'

Affluent merchants and aristocracy also deemed fortifications necessary during the religious turmoil and its aftermath. Pitkerro House was built in 1534 and is today subdivided into private flats. A visitor will find a keystone dated 1562 at Mains Castle in the heart of Caird Park. Claypotts Castle was constructed between 1569 and 1588 as a now-rare Z-plan house, with diagonally opposite towers. Its usefulness in enabling its defenders to fire broadsides across the castle attracted the family of conflict-friendly 'Bonnie Dundee' which purchased the ghost-patrolled Claypotts in 1601. And Dudhope Castle, seat of the hereditary constables of Dundee, was extended in 1580 to provide huge 'angle' towers to offer better sight for defenders. As to the push and shove of defence, it was beholden on all able men to turn out with their arms, 'when it sall happen the common bell to ring'.

In 1564 Mary, Queen of Scots stayed at Pitkerro House and by royal letter committed the right to the townspeople to inter their dead in the grounds of the demolished Franciscan monastery – now the Howff cemetery in the heart of the city's commercial centre. Among recorded Howff curiosities is a flat gravestone commemorating Walter Gourlay, his wife Elspeth Pie and their score of children:

> Epyte Pie, Here ly I. My Twentie bairnis.
> My Good Man and I. 1628.

More of a curiosity was that the Howff was used for meetings of merchants. By the mid-1500s the town had nine incorporated trades – baxters or bakers, cordiners or shoemakers, skinners or glovemakers, bonnetmakers, fleshers, dyers, hammermen, websters or weavers and waulkers or tailors. Until the late 1770s, they met and conducted business at the Howff gravestones of revered former members. Bakers were especially powerful as they had control over agricultural yields. A windmill near the shore at the foot of today's Union Street augmented the town's meagre burn water to drive their flour mills. Hammermen comprised every type of metal worker – including goldsmiths, cutlers, locksmiths, sword-makers and gunsmiths. Dundee had five sword-makers by 1585 and two others making hilts. Dundee pistols, of steel and brass, were fashionable and famous, and eight of thirty-five master craftsmen were gunmakers when the Hammermen Lockit Book was begun in 1587. David Wedderburn's *Compt Buik* entry for 3 October 1597 records sending a pair of pistols to Spain on the ship *St Andrews* and that John Scrymgeour was 'to sell the sam in Ingland or ony uther port he thinkis best to my profit'. Other organised trades included wrights, masons and slaters, who received their own charter from James VI in 1591. Most significantly, weavers, tailors, glovers and bonnetmakers contributed to Dundee's already mighty textiles trade – a manufacturing *tour de force* it would not relinquish for 500 years to come.

The town's growing importance can be gauged from its contribution to the controversial wedding of Mary to the Earl of Bothwell in 1567. Ten thousand pounds was levied on fourteen Scottish burghs to defray the cost of the wedding, of which Dundee's share of £1245 was second only to Edinburgh's £2500. Glasgow, yet an insignificant market town, contributed just £200. As the tragic royal events unfolded, Dundee was ordered in 1569 to send three vessels to 'serch and sek' for Bothwell, who had turned pirate after being exiled on the surrender of his wife. The Dundee ships, *James*, *Primrose* and *Robert*, formed the principal part of the fleet, which indicates that the sixteenth-century port boasted ships capable of force. The chase took them as far as the Orkneys but Bothwell managed to outrun his pursuers, eventually to be imprisoned in Denmark. Meanwhile, the unwelcome attention of English privateers in 1582 accounted for two vessels owned by Dundee businesswoman Agnes Cowty. The loss of her cargo was considered so great that a compensation claim was lodged with the infamous Elizabethan statesman Sir Francis Walsingham.

Plague returned in 1585 and lingered in Dundee for more than a year, causing many deaths, and probably pegging the town's population to around 5000. The severity of the disease forced the removal of the Overgate mint to Perth and encouraged Dundee's magistrates to hold their meetings in the open air at Magdalen Green. At such times, when disease dallied or wars worried, ordinary Dundonians also feared increased taxation, uncertainties over food supplies and rising bureaucracy.

The town council ruled every aspect of everyday life. A burgh law in October 1559, for example, threatened would-be adulterers with a punitive ducking in the Tay. Those 'apprehendit within this burgh sall for the first fault stand in the chokes of irone at the cross three houres in the maist notable tyme of day and thereafter had to the sea whair the gybit sall be set up and thrice duckat yairintill and again be brought to the cross and banished from the burgh for ever'. The warnings clearly passed over the bedsteads of the fun-loving citizenry. In 1589 additional prison accommodation for adulterers had to be provided by the council in St Mary's – and when a John Lyon escaped by digging a tunnel out of the building, he was ordered to dig his way back in again.

Even dress code was enforceable by law. Servants, men or women, wore canvas clothes 'and that they sall have no silk upon their clothes, except silk buttons and button-holes'. Labourers had to wear grey cloth for work, 'made in Scotland, and that their wyiffs and children wear the like'. Wealthier citizens were also constrained by burgh regulations: 'Na men within burgh that live be merchandise, unless they be in dignitie as Baillies, or gude worthy man of Council, shall wear clathis of silks, nor costly scarlet gowns, nor furrings.' You were what you wore – and women wore what was restrained.

The normal silence of historical sources is interrupted by snippets of the everyday life of merchant classes in sixteenth-century Dundee in David Wedderburn's *Compt Buik*. Wedderburn was a merchant and factor to the Scrymgeours. He was descended from one of the most notable Dundee families and his forebears included the religious reformer James Wedderburn, whose incendiary satires were performed at the town playfields at West Port before he was obliged by enraged churchmen to flee to Dieppe, 'wherein he carped roughly of the abuses and corruptions of the papists'. The *Compt Buik* shows that Dundee enjoyed ever-increasing trading links with continental Europe, its author describing business jaunts to Germany, Belgium, Holland and Russia. In the twenty years either side of 1600, the town imported flax, timber, iron, hemp and tar from the Baltic; wine, salt, vinegar, oils and dyes from the Spanish coast; wine and luxury goods from France. Landward trade was also important and Wedderburn recorded dealings in flax and yarn with the 'guidwives' of neighbouring Angus. But when his own womenfolk wanted the best silk for their petticoats, he sent abroad for the goods, ordering in 1598, '34 pounds of silk and lace and 118 hats lynnit with taffetie'. The scale of this purchase suggests personal items were probably bought for his extended family and friends, which was customary in the Elizabethan era.

On that subject, French claret had remained one of Dundee's most important imports, thanks to the demand created by religious and royal tables in the thirteenth century – a record 20,000 gallons was shipped to the town in 1620 alone. Certainly the good people would have required great dollops of the claret Wedderburn unloaded at the quayside when he recorded on 25 February 1597 the total 'ecclips of the sone'. Much to his fearful astonishment, 'betuix ten and ellevin houris before noon that day darkness overschaddowit the face of the hail earth,' a celestial phenomenon that struck fear into the souls of the inhabitants who fled 'mourning and lament-ing'. It was a day, he concluded, 'maist terrible and fairfull to all people young and auld. And nane persone lev and culd declair they ever hard or saw the lyk thame selffs in ony tyme preceiding.'

Wedderburn's record of the celestial phenomenon acts as a reminder of how, even in the late 1500s, everyday life was often shaped by a belief in occult influences and superstition. Even the crows and ravens took refuge in the Steeple, he added fearfully.

So, as the 1500s ended, Dundee was Scotland's leading port and third most important town after Edinburgh and Aberdeen. Between 1561 and 1571, seventy-nine of her ships traded with Holland, Belgium, France and Spain. Between 1580 and 1618, 259 vessels arrived from Baltic and Scandinavian ports. The town had a new school, constructed on the site of St Clement's in 1589, and the beginnings of a public library under the control of the town council. Most of its books had come from the Franciscan monastery, whose friars had accumulated richly illustrated manuscripts in the three centuries since the institution's founding by the Balliol family in the 1280s. During a severe famine in 1481, the monks had been forced to pawn sacred vessels and books in order to survive. Money, however, was donated by the Countess of Errol in return for a daily mass for her family. After-wards, books from the parent abbey of Lindores were re-housed in St Mary's. With the advent of the Reforma-tion the town council took over the remaining property of the Franciscans, moving their books to St Mary's, thereby creating the first municipal library. Some first editions in oaken boards were said to have been repaired by the Revd William Christeson (1560–1606) after sustaining damage in the English onslaught of 1548. Boasting 1800 volumes, Dundee's medieval library was a sign not only of the burgh's wealth, but of its literary and cultural renaissance as the 1500s turned into the 1600s.

The young St Andrews University graduate Timothy Pont may have witnessed the terrifying eclipse on his horseback journey to map Scotland, or perhaps borrowed a book on Ptolemy's travels from St Mary's library to aid his quest. Today, seventy-seven of his hand-drawn maps of Scotland survive on 138 fragile sheets in another great collection, the National Library of Scotland in Edinburgh. Pont probably arrived in Dundee shortly before 1600 and his map shows 'Dun-Tay' as a significantly sized town, with a complex layout of streets suggestive of a burgh of some importance. The towering Steeple is the most prominent building alongside named aristocratic mansions, such as Blackness, Balgay, Dryburgh and Clepington.

But the map is dominated by the town's busy harbour and the ships bobbing in the Firth. The river had remained constant as Dundee's focal point for its first five centuries. The town had prospered due to its harbour's stunning location for coastal and North Sea trade, closer to the Baltic than Edinburgh, by two days' sailing. Dundee was a conduit for imports from east-coast shipping and exports from town manufactures and its rich hinterland. Contributing to the blossoming economy, earlier disputes with Perth concerning jurisdiction over the Tay were settled in 1602 when both burghs agreed to share the river's passage, despite Dundee having overtaken Perth as a trading port.

Less successfully, Dundee quarrelled with the older

Trades Hall, c1870

Shopping at Greenmarket, c1890

Stewart Street, Lochee, c1890

Assembly Rooms, c1895

Demolition for Caird's offices, Ashton Place, c1900

Old Tay Bridge on c1900 postcard

Royal Arch and William IV Dock, c1900

Whaler leaving, c1900

Departure of whaler, c1912

Mary Slessor with her adopted son, 1906

Suffragette campaign, 1908

Mathers Hotel, c1920

Greenmarket and Shore Terrace, c1920

VOTE FOR
CHURCHILL

The Liberal and Anti-Socialist Candidate

OFFICIALLY SUPPORTED BY THE LIBERAL AND CONSERVATIVE ASSOCIATIONS OF DUNDEE.

For 15 Years Your Faithful Representative

WHAT MR CHURCHILL HAS DONE

He had the Fleet ready in the day of Britain's need.
He originated the Unemployment Insurance Scheme.
He smashed the Cattle Embargo.
He piloted successfully the Irish Treaty.
He has given unfailing attention to all Local Interests,

MAKE DUNDEE'S INFLUENCE COUNT
IN THE NATIONAL COUNCILS.

WOMEN ELECTORS!
Churchill Stands for Home and Family.

UNITE FOR STABILITY AND SOBER PROGRESS

CHURCHILL FOR DUNDEE

Churchill election leaflet, 1922

royal burgh over precedence in the Scottish Parliament, pointing out that it paid almost twice as much as Perth in taxation. Interestingly, the Dundee legation, sprinkled with powerful Wedderburns and Scrymgeours, also attempted to persuade a court of arbitration that Dundee was more ancient than Perth 'by hundreds of years'.

From that day to this, Perth has not had much idea of its antiquity. Although it is presently preparing celebrations for its 800th anniversary in 2010, if it spent less time in organising entertainment and more on research it would discover it was a burgh at least a century earlier, complete with a king in its castle and the Scots parliament in residence at times. When precedence was conferred on Perth in 1602, Dundee responded with a stinging accusation that the decree giving priority to its smaller rival was obtained 'by sinister means'. It probably was – though Dundee down the years has seldom required lessons in dubious diplomacy.

It is perhaps ironic that the expansion of the Howff graveyard ended in 1601. Shortly after, plague (or possibly typhus) struck the town once again, 'lingering in the closes, wynds and pends' until 1607. The disease plunged the life of the community into chaos, at a time when the nation was dithering after Elizabeth I's death and debating accession. Victims were stretchered to the Sickmen's Yard beyond the Seagate and left to die. Properties were isolated. Merchants and travellers were suspected of being infection carriers and parcels of flax were returned to rural hamlets. Ships from the Continent were held in quarantine in the estuary. Elections to the town council had to be cancelled. At times like this Dundee, like other burghs, could be a place of misery and despondency. Those of wealthier families, who could outrun the pestilence, looked back on poorer parts of the town where it was not worth counting the living, only the dead. And with luck the disease would not follow.

What was life like for the rich and poor of Dundee at the start of the seventeenth century? Around the harbour and marketplace, the lanes and wynds were cramped and crowded, filled with barefooted bairns, itinerant street-sellers, fortune tellers and petty thieves. Single-fronted, timber-framed houses were piled high behind frontages boasting haberdashers, butchers, bakers, cobblers, tailors, apothecaries, fishmongers and drapers. Carts carrying produce to market, flocks of sheep, laden horses and yelping dogs added to the noisy bustle. But Dundee in the early 1600s also boasted several fine stone-built merchant houses, churches, harbour warehousing, fortified mansions and castles. There was freedom of movement within and between the classes, and rich and poor lived cheek by jowl in the busy courts and closes linking harbour, marketplace and places of worship.

The Tay was the people's escape and playground. Here, children would watch barges carrying Kingoodie stone on the river, fishermen casting salmon nets and cargoes of flax, salt and coal unloading at the customs hall. In 1620 'anything up to twenty timber-laden ships might arrive in port' – a hint of Scotland's treeless landscape at the time. Ships crowded the dockside and merchants still used the river as their road. It would be another century before the turnpike to Perth opened up the Hawk Hill.

The best houses had narrow timber frontages but their interiors expanded like Dr Who's Tardis. Beyond the deceptive façade, a heavily-carved staircase led to a spacious first-floor gallery, the most important room in the house, with a further one or two floors above and a garret in the gable. The interior walls of the public rooms of the wealthiest homes were lined in oak, or hung with tapestries showing forest scenes or imagery work depicting biblical or classical stories. Ceilings were normally plastered or panelled. A modern chimneypiece surrounded a large hearth, around which the family would huddle on winter nights warmed by coal imported from the Forth or Newcastle. Floors were covered with woven rush mats; while carpets were kept for table coverings and for cloaking food cupboards. A solid 'joyned' table of oak or elm would be used in the principal public room, a smaller example kept in the parlour. Chairs, once reserved for the head of the family, were plentiful by the early 1600s and, by this time, some windows were glazed.

For those with wealth, this was a time to show it. 'In the houses of knights, gentlemen and merchantmen,' noted John Harrison in 1587, 'it is no geson [commonplace] to behold generally their great provision of tapestry, Turkey work, pewter, brass, fine linen and thereto costly cupboards of plate, worth five or six hundred or a thousand pounds.' But in less well-off seventeenth-century homes beds and tables, and even linen, were prized possessions and were formally bequeathed to their owners' loved ones. And Dundee's poorest always formed an unhealthy majority.

Even in the well-to-do homes of magistrates and merchants, bailies and burgesses, rooms and beds were allocated and shared as the family grew, as sleeping with the same sex was considered normal. Bedrooms were sparsely furnished, with a bed, blankets, feather bolster, curtains, hanging press and perhaps a small table to hold a water basin. Sheets and napery were plentiful. Decorated boxes held precious personal property, trinkets and small jewels. Bedrooms might also boast a polished steel mirror and closed stools, or pails, for toilet purposes. Putting this into the language of c.1600 Dundee, the chamber of Alexander Lovell, a modest merchant of Flukergait contained: 'the fedder bed and bowster, a water pot, a werdor [tent] bed and twa blankets, the mantill [bedcover] and sheets, the press, a silver spune, a towl, and twa servitors [linen napkins].'

This is the type of house that was owned by Provost James Halliburton, who presided in office for thirty-three years until 1588, and once led the men of Dundee to protect Perth's religious reformers against the Catholicising English. It is the type which provided lodgings for King James VI on his belated visit to Dundee in 1617, and which the prominent and influential Scrymgeour and Wedderburn families occupied. It was probably how the eminent doctor David Kinloch lived. Kinloch had escaped death at the hands of the Spanish Inquisition before being appointed court physician to King James. His death in 1617, fifteen years after being admitted as a burgess of Dundee, was marked by one of the most magnificent Howff tombs.

Kinloch's *De Hominis Procreatione*, published in 1596, made him the first Scottish writer on obstetrics – an honour for a town which also produced, 350 years later, the brilliant obstetrics pioneer Margaret Fairlie, Scotland's first ever woman professor. But in the Dundee of the 1600s, women's subordination was axiomatic. They were expected to possess myriad submissive virtues – among them modesty, obedience and silence – and domestic roles were rigidly divided by gender and reinforced by influential conduct books. There were exceptions, but most women had to depend on their husbands' interpretation of appropriate conduct. Access to education was limited – and most girls were not taught to write. Predestined for their future roles, some were even christened 'Silence'.

Girl power occasionally surfaced. It was the Dundee schoolteacher David Lindsay, then Bishop of Edinburgh, who was the target of Jenny Geddes' stool at St Giles in 1638, an act which provoked the double whammy of riot and revolution.

Status and reputation were everything – and available income gravitated towards the upper ranges of society. The working classes missed out. Theirs was a 'quarrelsome, gossiping life'. Men and women were often drunk or idle or both. Men maltreated women and obedience was considered the overriding duty of children – yet marriage could be sexually consummated by boys at fourteen and girls at twelve.

Religion dominated day-to-day life. Ministers enforced attendance at church and filled their sermons with images of disorder and corruption, tales of riots and robberies, and taunts about the indiscretion and impropriety of women who, nonetheless, produced babies at the rate of one a year. Houses were damp and unhygienic, piped water hopelessly inadequate and streets filthy and reeking of dung. In 1591, the town hangman also became Dundee's first public street-cleaner.

But badness was outweighed by propriety and the Protestant work ethic. The engine of Scotland's economic strength remained her eastern seaboard, and by the 1640s Dundee was second only to Edinburgh in size and wealth. It had a population of nearly 12,000. Its market and port were bustling, and opulent new houses lined its principal streets. It imported claret by the gallon, 'Inglis drinking beir' by the barrel, and punched above its weight in the level of taxes and customs it paid to the national coffers. And when, during a time of relative peace between Scotland and England, Charles I granted the town's Great Charter in 1641, confirming all its historic privileges, the future seldom looked more promising for the bustling community. In a spirit of renewed confidence, the town council in the same year made a bold attempt to subsume the Hilltown into Dundee's boundaries. In reprisal, Lord Dudhope threatened to make the Hilltown an independent town, one with a rival market which would bleed Dundee's commercial heart. The power struggle was cut short when Dudhope was killed at the Battle of Marston Moor in 1644.

Dudhope's death was an omen. The English Civil Wars proved disastrous for Dundee.

James Graham, Marquis of Montrose, first laid siege to the Protestant-leaning town in 1644, but its defences stalled the royalist advance. The persistent Montrose was more successful the following year, capturing the town's guns on the rocky outcrop of Corbie Hill and turning them on the defenders. The cost in fire damage, theft and other destruction was considerable and an appeal to the Scottish Parliament, which described the town as 'fearfully defaced and disabled', won a sympathetic handout of £54,000, equivalent to around £7 million today.

Famously, much worse was to follow. Parliament's decision to execute Charles I in 1649 was met with horror in Scotland. North of the border his son was recognised as Charles II and crowned at Scone in 1651, enraging the Parliamentary leader Oliver Cromwell. On 26 August 1651, forces under Cromwell's general George Monk withdrew their siege ladders from Perth and 7000 Puritan troops, swords in hand, psalms on their lips, marched down the Carse of Gowrie to demand the surrender of Dundee. They took with them 'three great guns and mortar pieces' which were reinforced outside Dundee's walls by 'platforms and batteries for about ten guns brought from the ships'. The town, which had been previously 'warned' by a volley of shots from the Parliamentary frigate *Speaker*, rejected demands to surrender. Instead, according to a contemporary account, 'The Governor of the town, Sir Robert Lumsdaine, "desired" Monck and his army to lay down their arms and "conform to the King's Majesty's declaration".'

How ironic that within the space of just five years Dundee's siege-fatigued inhabitants found themselves facing the guns of both Cavalier and Roundhead generals. And yet the tradition that Monk's assault on Dundee was a protracted attack needs to be addressed. Robert Mudie (1822) and James Chalmers (1842), for example, claimed the siege 'lasted five or six weeks' and this impression passed to later histories. There is no evidence of a drawn-out engagement in the account recorded by Monk's secretary, however:

'Sept 1, About four o'clock in the morning our great guns began to play before Dundee. The enemy for two or three hours answered us gun for gun, besides small shot from their works, til such time as large breaches were made in two of their considerable forts . . . Mr Hane the engineer played the mortar piece. About eleven o'clock the signal was given, and breaches being made into the enemy's forts on the east and west sides of the town, our men entered, and after about half an hour of hot dispute, diverse of the enemy retreated to the church and steeple, and amongst the rest the Governor, who

71

was killed with between four and five hundred soldiers and townsmen . . . There was killed of ours Capt. Hart and about 20 soldiers, and as many wounded.'

Monk's doctor and eventual biographer Thomas Gumble also confirmed the immediacy of the assault: 'Both horse and foot fell on, and after a short, sharp resistance, he mastered the town.'

Chivalric conventions of military siege were put into practice. A garrison that refused a summons to surrender had relinquished its right of safe passage and could expect no mercy. Monk was within his rights to allow his men to pillage the town 'without licence' for one day. Instead, his troops were probably engaged in three days of killing and burning, sweeping through the town, overwhelming its defenders and putting them to the sword – combatants and citizenry, women, children and priests. The head of poor Governor Lumsden was said to have adorned a spike on an abutment on the Debenham's side of the Steeple, a 'point' overlooking today's skateboarders who claim the area with, pleasingly, the city churches' blessing for their activities. Dr David Small, writing in 1792, mentioned that the spike remained visible for a century.

In describing the terror that Dundee was subjected to, local histories frequently claim that the town was made an example of in the manner that the normally restrained Oliver Cromwell infamously put Drogheda to the sword in the summer of 1649. Yet, given the conventions of warfare, Monk's siege of Dundee was probably not regarded as an atrocity at the time, just as the slaughter in the Irish town, in which 3500 people died – including the governor, who was bludgeoned to death with his own wooden leg – was not reported as a massacre. A besieged town which refused terms to surrender could expect no mercy, and Dundee got none.

The number of dead in Dundee probably reached around 1500, or an eighth of its population, but this figure included religious and monarchist refugees. An irony is that the local soldiers who met the full force of the Parliamentary onslaught probably fought alongside Oliver Cromwell in the rout of royalist forces at Marston Moor in 1644. The Earl of Dalhousie's regiment had seven troops of horse, each comprising eighty men, at Cromwell's command. Alongside, the Angus Regiment, commanded by Viscount Dudhope, comprised a regiment of foot probably drawn from Dundee. 'God made them as stubble to our swords,' Cromwell wrote to Speaker Lenthall at the House of Commons after the battle. Within a year, Charles I had surrendered to the Scottish army, and so the wheels turned full circle and Scotland became Parliament's enemy.

The impact of Monk's siege was not limited to human casualties or damage to the town's built environment. Of the 159 children born within the eight months following the assault, twenty-five were posthumous to fathers killed in battle. Nor did the presence of so many young soldiers in the protectoral garrison pass unnoticed. Among marriages in Dundee over the next six years, sixty-six were to English soldiers and no fewer than 255 baptisms were to English fathers. In William Blain's 1946 novel *Witch's Blood*, later a successful play, Elspet Rankyne is raped and made pregnant by an English trooper in the aftermath of the siege. She was neither the first nor the last raped woman to be denied justice – but probably one of the few to be burned at the stake for her protest.

Several stories from Monk's 'massacre' require scrutiny. We have previously noted that skeletons 'from the siege' found from time to time in the vicinity of the historic Steeple – the 'dead bodies promiscuously thrown into pits dug on the spot' – were most likely decent burials in St Mary's ancient cemetery. Soldiers and citizenry siege victims were probably properly disposed of in what remained of the medieval kirkyard or in the Howff. Although there are 1451 recorded interments in the Howff, many more people were previously buried there, their bones trampled down every generation or so to allow graves to be reused.

As we have noted, it is doubtful whether the siege was prolonged. It is also possible that it was not considered at the time the massacre painted by local histories. But the mightiest of myths surrounds Monk's 'treasure' ships. Thomas Gumble's biography of General Monk relates how a fleet of around sixty vessels was commandeered by Parliamentary forces to carry away plunder from the sacked port. Gumble states that a storm left the fleet scuppered on the estuarial sands, depositing some 200,000 gold coins, and gold and silver artefacts, firing the imaginations of treasure-hunters periodically ever since. In 1925 the city's Prohibition MP Edwin Scrymgeour proposed that the gold and silver, if discovered, could help Dundee's mass unemployed. Trial borings were sunk to a depth of eighty feet without result. As recently as 2002, *The Sun* newspaper blazed a headline 'The Hunt for Monck's £2.5 Billion Treasure' as yet another salvage team prepared to investigate the supposed sinking.

Into the basket of Dundee mythology this confused heritage of facts must go. The only near-contemporary source for the treasure ships story is Dr Gumble, physician to Monk during the Dundee siege and his biographer twenty years later in 1671. By then, however, Gumble was aligned to the court of Charles II, and his book was dedicated to the restored king. Gumble certainly recorded that the plunder in Dundee was 'the best' to be had in the three nations defeated by Cromwell's army, but his insistence on adding the moralistic epitaph 'Ill got, soon lost' to the treasure story suggests that it was no more than a rounding off to suit Restoration sensitivities. It would not have been politically correct to present cloying royalist readers with a devastating loss of royalist treasures. Neither would printed triumphalism over the massacre of citizens and clergy in Dundee have sat well with a religiously tolerant king. In any case Gumble would have been all too well aware that it was the iron-fisted Monk, realising that the rebuilding of the country required a stable monarchy, who engineered Charles II's return to the throne in 1660.

Gumble's biography was penned for loyalty and wit as much as for historical accuracy. In fact, a 1712 reprint was peddled to raise funds for the royalist Stuart cause prior to the Jacobite uprising. Perhaps the only glimmer of truth to be teased from the tale is that the town harbour was capable of holding so many ships.

Some backward-looking prejudices returned on the restoration of Charles II in 1660. Supposed witches, especially, were persecuted in their local communities and Grizzel Jaffray was immortalised as Dundee's witch long before the vampire-slaying Buffy or broomstick-flying Harry Potter materialised.

We know little of Jaffray's life and only a snapshot of her death. She was probably the wife of James Butcher, a brewer, who lived in a house in Thorter Row, in the old

Overgate. But we cannot be sure she brewed up potions from the eye of newt and toe of frog. Council records show that on 11 November 1667 she was sent to trial in Dundee on suspicion of the 'horrid crime of witchcraft'. Whether the accusation was supported with evidence we do not know. No matter. The Privy Council in Edinburgh appointed seven officials from neighbouring Angus to investigate her case and gave them weighty judicial powers. Jaffray was found guilty. She was tied to a stake and burned in front of a huge and smugly satisfied crowd. It is likely that the 'entertainment' began with the poor woman being strangled, as was tradition, the prospect of which probably encouraged her outburst on the point of death to implicate several other women. Her sorcery was captured in rhyme by *The City Echo*, a short-lived satirical magazine from the Edwardian era:

> 'Come out, come out, foul witch Jaffray,
> Or e'er the night return,
> Thy body wirried at the stake,
> In flames o' hell shall burn.

> 'Come out, come out, Grizzel Jaffray,
> Come out, come out, they cry;
> Thy soul is barter'd to the de'il,
> Thou hast the evil eye.'

History is often as murky as a witch's brew, but Jaffray's burning seems to have been an individual and tragic case. Although Dundee's burgh chamberlain calculated in 1590 the cost of having a witch put to death as £5.16s.2d Scots, which included 'twa tar barrels', the town appears to have been the most reluctant in the region to execute accused women. Other than the occasion when 'a company of witches' was burned at the stake in Dundee in 1569 at the height of persecutions, Jaffray's death seems to be an isolated incident among a clutch of witch persecutions in neighbouring Angus, Perthshire and Fife – three executions on the South Inch in Perth in 1598 and three more on the North Inch in 1623, nine in Forfar between 1656 and 1662, and sixteen executions in Pittenweem alone between 1597 and 1705 from a total of around 300 cases in Fife.

Where willowy fact meets wayward fiction is over the legend of Jaffray's child. According to tradition, Jaffray's son, the captain of a small vessel, just happened to sail into the estuary on the day of his mother's execution. On inquiring about the commotion, and on being told of the distressing circumstances, he set sail immediately and vowed never to return to Dundee. A. H. Millar, Dundee's former city librarian, believed a son could have existed and suggested that Jaffray had come from Aberdeen to Dundee. No evidence of this could be found, nor any that Jaffray had a son. More likely she came to Dundee from a rural community, where it was common for girls and women to practise superstitious rites, often connected to religious or agricultural festivals.

Thomas Tucker, an English tourist who did arrive in the harbour in the summer of 1665, noted the community's depressed state as it struggled to recover from the 1651 siege and the fear and vengeance that inevitably followed: 'The towne of Dundee was sometime a towne of riches and trade, but in the many recontres it has mett withall in the time of domestick commotions and her obstinacy and pride of late years rendring her a prey to the soldier have much shaken and abated her former grandeur.' The obstinate, proud town was 'not glorious' though 'yett not contemptible'.

Exacerbating the town's stalled and fragmented development was the political turmoil which brought the seventeenth century to a close. There was widespread anger and violent opposition to the deposition of James VII of Scotland and II of England by the Dutch prince William of Orange. With Scotland's national identity under threat, the rise of Jacobism was centred on the military adventurism of John Graham, Viscount Dundee, who raised his standard at Dudhope Castle on his way to his army's victory at the Battle of Killiecrankie in 1689. But Bonnie Dundee, who had plundered, burned and butchered his way across the country, did not survive his greatest victory and the 'Bonnie' nomenclature passed to the town of his birth. As it was put so gloriously among the incorrigible Good Things in W. C. Sellar and R. J. Yeatman's *1066 And All That,* 'The Scots continued to squirl and hoot at the Orange, and a rebellion was raised by the memorable Viscount Slaughterhouse (the Bonnie Dundee) and his Gallivanting Army. Finally Slaughterhouse was defeated at the Pass of Ghilliekrankie and the Scots were all massacred at Glascoe, near Edinburgh.' Aye . . .

One important local history concluded that after the Monk depredations 'in under twenty years the town had repaired and rebuilt itself'. The surviving records suggest otherwise. The despair and destruction brought by the Montrose and Monk sackings left the mood despondent and the population static. Trade stalled and economic recovery was sluggish. In hard cash, Dundee paid around eleven per cent of Scotland's tax assessment before 1645, but only about four per cent by the end of the century. In other words, it did not have money to pay for new housing or grand civic buildings, apart from a much-needed hospital. Prior to the 1651 siege, an average of ten vessels a week traded with Baltic ports. For the three years afterwards no ships sailed there, or made the 850-mile trip to the favoured trading town of Danzig – a German port to which Dundee would have just historical cause to offer twinning links. Dundee's post-siege exports were half of what they were in 1591, its coastal trade only one sixth.

When the Dutch artist and traveller Johannes Slezer drew Dundee from the east and north in 1678 for his *Theatrum Scotiae*, he left an image of a compact town, with a harbour contained within a neat sea wall, and handsome houses rising above it. It looks pretty. It seems prosperous. Slezer was taken in. What he illustrated was largely the Dundee of the 1630s. Having been attacked and pillaged, the town did not develop for half a century. Survivors of the siege could still cross it on foot in ten minutes.

5

1700 TO 1800
REBELLION AND RENAISSANCE

Eighteenth-century Dundee began with a political rebellion and ended with a cultural revolution. But the early years of the 1700s offer no hint of the transformation to come, only the continuing dearth of the previous decade. England's anti-Gallic prejudices and the arrival of new products through trading clauses in the Treaty of Union in 1707 served to ruin indigenous Dundee industries, affected its trade with the Dutch and French, destroyed the town's manufacturing morale and placed its council 'in the throes of bankruptcy'. Whatley (1993) noted a Charles Gray, combmaker, asking the town council if he could fill the vacant post as jailer because the 1707 union had 'broke' his business.

Adding to the economic turmoil was a famine which gripped much of Scotland, causing untold suffering among poorer people unable, like wealthier classes, to leave a record of their distress. The *Statistical Account* of Dundee, published later in the century, spoke for them by recalling, 'Our staple manufacture was the spinning and weaving of coarse woollens, called plaiding. They were sent to the Dutch market. By the loss of our Dutch and French privileges so completely since the union no remainder of it is to be found.' The scars of seventeenth-century hostilities had not healed. Little money could be spared anywhere for civic improvements or substantial new building. Revenues from taxes levied on traded goods at Dundee's market fell by half between 1707 and 1710 and the town was burdened by increasing debt.

As the seventeenth turned into the eighteenth century the people of Dundee were also drawn into the debate over Scotland's governance. The town council largely supported the claim to the throne of the exiled Stuarts and was probably involved in the planned but abandoned rebellion in 1708, when a French fleet reached as far as the Forth, as well as the 1715 Jacobite uprising, which it commemorated with a drum salute and proclamation of the Old Pretender at the Market Cross. James Stuart himself arrived on horseback in the town at the head of 300 marching clansmen in January 1716, the bells of the Steeple cracking from the exuberance with which they were rung in his honour. The people 'crowded around him in great numbers' to catch a glimpse of 'the adventurer who had come among them' in the way that city centre crowds today might respond to a PR visit by a *Big Brother* housemate – the young and enthused pressing to the front, the bemused behind and the indignantly disinterested carrying on their business regardless. But by then Stuart had suffered defeat at Sheriffmuir and the momentum of rebellion was fading.

It is said that the Old Pretender spent the night in the Seagate town house where Adam Duncan, later Admiral Duncan, victor of the Battle of Camperdown, was born fifteen years later. Less believable is the story that gold sent to the Jacobite leader by the King of Spain was lost in the Tay when the ship carrying it to Dundee foundered . . . a tale probably muddled with the Monk 'treasure'. However, such anecdotes must have helped to lift the

citizenry out of the new-century doldrums, while en-
hancing the sunken fortunes of the unsuspecting estuarial
sands.

Oddly, the visit to Dundee in 1724 by the government
spy Daniel Defoe reflected the town in a favourable light.
Five years after writing *Robinson Crusoe*, Defoe noted that
Dundee was 'populous, full of stately houses and handsome streets, with a large market-place in the middle'.
The writer also noted that Dundee had become again
'one of the best trading towns in Scotland'. While Defoe's
testimony implies partial recovery, it provides no real
evidence of wealth-generation or the physical expansion
of the burgh in the early part of the century. He recorded,
for example, that the town's harbour was 'indifferent' –
and Dundee's harbour was its economic barometer. Simi-
larly, construction in 1732 of William Adam's Town
House in the High Street is often cited as a sign of Dundee's recovering fortunes. It was certainly one of the
finest civic buildings in Scotland, not least because its
arcaded pillars provided shelter during rainfall – but it
was as much pragmatic replacement as aesthetic addi-
tion. Adam had previously reported to the town council
that the old tollbooth was so out of plumb that it was a
danger to the citizens. The Town House was never intended as a tourist attraction. Its interior provided two
rooms for bad debtors and three 'for those guilty of notorious crimes'. An eyewitness recalled looking up at the
bars of the prison on its third floor and seeing female
prisoners 'at the windows with the glass part open. In the
evenings they could get a blink of the sun, and often held
converse with friends on the street, getting the news.'

In fact, the Town House apart, there was little civic
improvement in the first half of the century to transform

the dark aftermath of Monk's siege. The town's progress was painfully slow.

Development was further impaired by the ramifications of the political turmoil in the middle of the century. Almost inevitably, Dundee was occupied in 1745 by the Jacobites, to whom a lukewarm reception was delivered when they locked up Provost Duncan (father of the admiral) in his own gaol. The council's change of political hat meant the Highlanders were regarded this time as undesirable. The belligerent reaction to their plundering stay in Dundee prompted the cautious *Caledonian Mercury* to make a plea for peace: 'May the Lord avert a Civil War, and powerfully protect our dear native Country.' And when, in 1747, the town council organised public rejoicings and agreed to offer the Freedom of the town to 'Butcher' Cumberland after his harsh repression of the rebellion, the gold box it presented to the general bankrupted the town once again.

A century after the grim victorious veterans of the New Model Army had marched away, Dundee remained fragile. When a visitor viewed it in 1746, the Howff cemetery was still its northern boundary and the streets did not extend to present-day Perth Road, or much beyond the Overgate. The same eyewitness reported the population at roughly 6000, half of what it was during its flourishing renaissance prior to the English Civil Wars. The *Statistical Account* noted, 'At the cross, in the principal street in the town, there were in 1746 not above four or five houses completely built of stone, all the rest were partly of wood.'

It painted a picture of a town in depression: 'No shop rented at more than £2, the retailers who rented them were generally poor, three shops at the cross were entirely shut.'

It also captured the low morale of the people. If one of the town's two churches was full, the other was empty. As providence would have it, the prayers of troubled Dundee were answered.

The timely shift to coarse linen manufacture after the ruination of Dundee's cloth industry restored the town's fortunes. A new bleachfield was laid out for hand-spun flax in 1732, and while most handlooms remained close to running water in the rural northern hinterland, the first two hand-weaving factories for the low-status linen called osnaburg were noted in Dundee in 1742. The benefits of clustering handloom production quickly became evident and the pace of transfer from cottage to factory accelerated. Supported by government bounty, raw flax imports from Riga and St Petersburg increased and a rush to establish new water-driven looms occurred. In just thirty years – between 1740 and 1770 – the two pioneering hand-weaving factories in the town had mushroomed to more than seventy.

The dramatic expansion of linen production resulted in an economic leap forward in spinning and weaving communities across Scotland. By 1791, eight million yards of linen were being exported annually from Dundee alone. The *Statistical Account* recorded the town's cloth production that year in a quartet of itemised products:

Brown linen, osnaburg, 25 inches wide, used 'for clothing the Negroes of the West Indies'.

Bleached linen, in imitation of the 'sheeting of Russia and shirting of Germany'.

Sail Cloth, which could be had 'in point of strength, fabric and appearance equal to any manufacture in England'.

Cotton bagging, forty to forty-two inches wide, for bagging cotton products.

The following chapter scrutinises the reference to 'Negro' clothing and the dramatic increase of Dundee linen cargoes to the slave plantations of the New World. But the slave trade was brought closer to home in 1777, when David Wedderburn returned from Jamaica with a negro called David Knight, who claimed that, due to Britain's rejection of slavery, he was due wages from his employer. The case came before the sheriff of Perth, who ruled that slave laws had no validity. Wedderburn's appeal to the Court of Session against the Perth decision was heard before a panel of judges. In a historic judgment, the court concluded that the slave laws of Jamaica were unjust, pronounced slavery to be against the law in Scotland and set Knight at liberty. In deciding that any slave who set foot in Scotland was free, the Scottish judges were courageously ahead of their time. Britain did not outlaw slavery until 1807.

Meanwhile, the rural population flooded into the town for work. There was an explosive rise in population and rapid diversification of associated trades to support and sustain the linen industry and its workforce. By the second half of the 1700s the town boasted factories producing soap, rope, candles, sugar, snuff, footwear, hats and clothes. By 1792, thirty-two people were employed as tanners of local leathers and hides, twelve for dressing leather, 150 for making shoes and boots for export and 200 for the town's footwear consumption. With town tanneries meeting local requirements, there was no reason to import leather and few references to it are seen in surviving records.

Another new venture was the production of coloured and white thread, which employed over 1000 people in seven factories, though this figure included outreach workers and suppliers in other parts of Scotland. The father of Fanny Wright, the anti-slavery campaigner, was a Dundee thread manufacturer, but an attempt to manufacture cotton – the other staple of the slave trade – failed. What shipping records do reflect is the renewed commercial confidence which prompted the town's entrepreneurs to purchase the aptly-named merchant-man *Dundee* from London, to rig her as a whaling vessel, and to set her sailing in 1753 for the hitherto unvisited northern whaling grounds. The *Dundee* returned with '143 casks containing blubber of four whales', representing, when taken with government bounty, a good return for the fledgling Dundee Whale Fishing Company.

Significant investment in linen, along with these new ventures, made considerable demands on the port. Their success encouraged shipbuilding and ship repairing, ship chandlering and the recruitment and retention of a growing harbourside workforce. So many petitions were presented to Dundee town council for permission to build ships next to the pier that in 1753 the cash-strapped authority cleverly decreed that no one could construct any vessel 'without first paying four shillings Scots to the council for each ton of ship to be built'.

By the 1760s the town's harbour was showing a profit and had 'usurped Perth as the navigable river's principal port'. By 1792 it could boast '116 vessels, navigated by 698 men', among which the quartet of wooden-hulled whaling ships dispatched to Greenland that year represented the first significant presence of a fully-fledged whaling industry in the town, and a huge investment by the standards of the eighteenth century. One ship alone was worth as much as David Dale's New Lanark mills in 1786 and matched the £5000 spent on the famous Belper cotton mill in the north of England in 1793. For the next century titanic profits would be reaped from whaling's cruel adventurism.

A handful of new companies to emerge at this time were to become familiar names. Shipbuilders Gourlay, founded as Dundee Foundry in 1790, sent some remarkable vessels down their slipway over the subsequent century. The Dundee, Perth & London Shipping Company was launched from two smaller shipyards in 1792 before expanding to become formidable shipowners in the 1820s when US trade demanded ocean-going vessels. Keiller's, later the marmalade kings, opened their first confectionery in 1797 – although the name James Keiller & Son was not adopted until the 1820s. It is probably to Janet Keiller, aged fifty-three in 1790, and her sweetie shop in Seagate, that we owe the creation of the firm that stocked the country's breakfast tables for two centuries and became one of Britain's most famous commercial families. The young firm perhaps invested in the Dundee Sugar Refining Company, established in 1770. Sarah Wiedemann, mother of the poet Robert Browning, was the daughter of its first manager. Above all, the manufacture of coarse linens dominated. On the back of its trade with the Americas, linen output tripled between 1773 and 1777 alone as the town briskly exploited transatlantic markets.

The mid-century return of economic prosperity and increasing money supply fixed physical improvements in the minds of the town council. Work was carried out to pave the Nethergate and mend smaller streets. Records show the council debating whether to purchase the town's first street lighting and, in a desire to improve hygiene, organising improved 'rubbish bin' uplift: 'The Council appoint the town drummer to go through the town ordering ye haill inhabitants upon every Monday and Saturday before twelve o' clock to raik all the dung and nastiness upon the high streets opposite their possessions and cause to put the same in little heaps so as it may be carried away.' Regarded today as Scotland's recycling city, Dundee no longer employs a drummer, but none-theless pioneered the composting of 'little heaps' of botanical waste in the 1980s.

There was also a boom in building. Grand civic new-comers in the second half of the eighteenth century included the Trades Hall in Murraygate (1776, unforgiv-ably demolished in 1878), a new slaughterhouse (1777), the Union Hall in High Street (1783) and Trinity House at Yeaman Shore (1790). Several new churches were built, including the graceful St Andrew's (1772), and of most importance, a new thoroughfare, Castle Street, was blasted out of Castlehill in 1783 to link flax factories to the shore. Crichton Street was laid out the same year, and Couttie's Wynd widened to allow horse-drawn carts access to the harbour. Milne's Buildings, in the Nethergate, laid out in 1788 and still with us, became the town residence of gentry released from hinterland 'culture and plantation'.

Importantly, the founding of the town's first bank in 1763 made available capital to promote new ventures and expansion. These included Dundee's first proper hos-pital, opened in King Street in 1798 as a dispensary of medicines to bring townspeople a measure of relief. Soon designated Dundee Infirmary, its early story is of a strug-gle for funds, of roll-calls to deter escapees, porridge and ale for breakfast, beer for lunch, of nurses fighting with patients and a matron who kept hens and a pig. In its first year it had forty-five in-patients, of whom five died. It had one bath.

As former hamlets and mansioned estates swelled into seething suburbs, all the town's medieval ports except the Cow Gate were removed to allow free movement of traffic. Land was reclaimed from the Tay to form new docks. In other areas, much of the medieval town was swept away to allow for improvement schemes. The wall containing Dundee in Slezer's map at the start of the century was no longer hemming in the town by Crawford's plan of 1777. Thomas Pennant, a visitor in 1772, described Dundee as a well-built town, estimated the population at around 14,000, praised the 'commodious' harbour where he counted seventy ships, and noted the presence of an early and sizeable whale ship of 264 tons. Not even Samuel Johnson's hostile description of Dundee as a 'dirty, despicable town' a year later in 1773 could deflect from a half-century of quiet, determined progress.

That is not to say that efforts to transform from medieval to modern solved or obliterated all of Dundee's problems – or that Johnson did not have a point. According to the 1793 *Statistical Account*, eighteenth-century lanes and streets were 'uncommonly narrow', the dwellings 'too close', the workers lived in houses 'by half dozens', the water supply was 'very inadequate' and the smallpox 'often epidemical and fatal'. Communications between towns and villages presented considerable difficulties, not least along muddied, potholed tracks. Jean Kinloch's predicament was probably not untypical when she wrote from Dundee in February 1759: 'I am determined not to go to Edinburgh. I am averse to travelling in a stage coach.' As well as profitable peaks, there were also manufacturing troughs resulting, for example, in meal riots in 1772 and 1773. Nobody liked ships leaving with grain when there were local deficiencies. But modern Dundee was at last taking shape.

By the end of this fascinating half-century of progress, Dundee boasted a population of 25,000. The town now stretched to the Hilltown to the north, Blackness to the west and Craigie to the east. It had become a manufacturing and finishing metropolis for coarse linen, no longer supplying the Continent's soldiers, but clothing slaves on American cotton plantations. Sister industries exported leather, threads, hats, soaps, barley, wheat and salmon, fashionably packed in ice for London markets. The harbour had been enriched by extension and modernisation and could receive ocean-going ships up to 300 tons. New vessels, rapidly increasing in size, were built on its quayside, and by 1792 the port was home to 116 ships and half a dozen yards.

If Dundee's links to the slave trade require historical revision, so too does its part in Scotland's eighteenth-century Enlightenment. Arthur Herman's otherwise excellent *The Scottish Enlightenment* (2001) claims that 'Glasgow, Aberdeen and Edinburgh were the triple well-springs of the modern mind'. To discount the changing character and mushrooming momentum of Dundee's scholarly eighteenth-century transformation is to render it a gross disservice. If the term Enlightenment is conceptual shorthand for liberty of thinking, then Dundee was not the town burning witches in these times. It was a forward-thinking regional centre, in which immense progress and achievements were made and where a refashioning of cultural awareness accelerated as the century progressed.

Dundee's increased cultural provision included a new subscription library, literary, debating and art societies and a network of 'newspapers and lawyers, booksellers and confectioners, the four chief characteristics of a capital'. It was, according to architectural historian Charles McKean, a flourishing town comfortable with itself, not tempted like other urban centres to construct a 'new' town within its boundaries. One can sense a civic pride and a depth of intellectual life that was not present decades before.

Into this intellectually acquisitive society of ambitious manufacturers, merchants, shopkeepers, bankers, lawyers and tradesmen entered a vibrant press. Probably the first publication printed in the town was *The Dundee Weekly Intelligencer*, a collection of sermons and polemicist tracts compiled by Henry Galbraith in 1759. After Galbraith, Thomas Colville printed religious pamphlets from Kay's Close (later Whitehall Crescent), as well as launching the periodicals *Dundee Repository* in 1793 and the *Dundee Magazine* in 1815 (by which time the first history of Dundee by John Berwick had been published). Among other notable eighteenth-century printed works was the *Dundee Register* of 1783, the forerunner of the much loved and much missed *Dundee Directories*, which last appeared in 1974. Colville also printed *The Courier*, launched a year after Waterloo as a cautious, conservative riposte to the radical *Advertiser* of 1801.

At least two booksellers had premises in the High Street, another at old Marketgate and one in Flukergait – and there was a newspaper room in the Trades Hall. In 1782 the renowned poet Robert Nicoll, the 'second Burns', established a bookshop in Castle Street, where he employed the father of Thomas Hood. The phenomenally successful poet and humorist Hood spent part of his youth working as an apprentice in the shop. He tutored the son of Admiral Duncan for a time, and wrote his first story for the *Dundee Magazine* in 1816. Robert Mudie, founder of London's celebrated Mudie Lending Library, kept a neighbouring bookshop, but is better known locally for *Dundee Delineated*, a history of the town published in 1822 which past and present local historians value as an important record of the early community.

A revolution of thinking was almost inevitable. As communities began to question parliamentary abuses, Dundee gained a reputation for radical reform, like others flirting with the hopes and aspirations of the French Revolution in 1792. The potent mix of internationally-minded merchants, forward-thinking manufacturers and a growing middle class was bound to develop an outward-looking, inquisitive mindset. Among groups embracing the ferment of new ideas were the Revolution Society, the Friends of Liberty, the Society of Friends of the People, the Friends of the Constitution and the Rational Society. In June 1790 the Whig Club in Dundee sent a message to the French National Assembly praying that their revolutionary action 'would be universally followed' and congratulating them 'on their enlightened view of liberty'. In 1791 members of the Dundee Revolution Society pledged themselves to the 'rights of men' and the abolition of the slave trade – a campaign not welcomed by nervous linen merchants. In 1792 a Friends of Liberty branch was formed in the town. A year later, its secretary Thomas Palmer was tried for sedition and sentenced to seven years in Botany Bay for arranging the printing and distribution of George Mealmaker's *Address to the People*, an inflammatory pamphlet on parliamentary reform. Mealmaker, the Dundee weaver who led the United Scotsmen movement, was sentenced to fourteen years, and died in the Australian penal colony.

Palmer's pamphlet also urged the public to read Thomas Paine's radical writing. In 1793 the Dundee thread merchant James Wright arranged for a cheap printed edition of Paine's *Ages of Reason* and sold more than 1000 copies. Wright was in regular contact with the famous author, whose *Rights of Man* in 1791 was a justification of the French Revolution. Wright's daughter Frances, growing up in Milne's Buildings in the Nethergate, became a champion of Paine's ideology. Ahead of her time, Fanny Wright is today regarded as one of the mothers of women's emancipation in the United States, where she drew thousands to hear her reformist views. Back in her native Dundee it was little wonder that riot – the symptom of frustration and injustice – was never far below the surface.

Paine's incendiary writings and the sniff of revolution abroad led to a period of bad-tempered public turbulence in Dundee. As prices for food and property rose, shops were looted, well-to-do homes attacked and ships laden with grain prevented from sailing. A meal mob attacked Mylnfield House at Invergowrie, whose owner, Thomas Mylne, had been exporting corn, but met their match in swarthy farm workers wielding sickles. In another incident in November 1792, a mob gathered in High Street with the solemn intention of planting a Tree of Liberty to mark the Revolutionary Army's attack on Brussels. A 1000-strong crowd then marched on the Town House and forced Provost Alexander Riddoch to dance round a bonfire built in the market place, doffing his cap to the success of the Revolution. The next day the humiliated provost threw the tree in the town's jail. His action precipitated a week of rioting, quelled only when troops were sent into the town to regain control.

Riddoch (1745–1822) was the most notorious, controversial and ambitious figure of eighteenth-century public life in Dundee. By his early thirties he was a successful merchant and had won a position on Dundee town council. He remained its unmovable rock for the next forty years, during which time he was involved in forty-three separate property transactions in Dundee, many of them controversial and accusingly reported to be designed to line his own pockets. Riddoch also lucratively loaned money to the town when its civic coffers were empty. He negotiated, traded, pulled strings, coerced and controlled his way through almost a half-century of autocratic rule. When he died, he left a wife bedecked in expensive clothes and jewels, a house in the Nethergate 'furnished with the best of furniture, with silver plate, paintings, books and prints' (now the Clydesdale Bank), not to mention £13,000, or £1 million today, in hard cash.

Riddoch is an important figure in this history as he was a brash newcomer to civic life who did much to oust rock-solid guildry and old mercantile families from positions of power. Not until the early years of the twentieth century would the new shopkeeper classes, which he represented, give up hard-won seats on the municipal council to the jute barons. And it was Riddoch, the self-perpetuating oligarch whose gravestone lies lamentably damaged in the Howff, who was responsible for propelling Dundee into the next century when he commissioned Robert Stevenson to improve the town's harbour. In response, Riddoch's enemies commissioned rival engineer Thomas Telford to produce a more extensive scheme of harbour improvements, which eventually transformed the waterfront.

As history showed time and time again, when its port

was successful and expanding its sea-borne exchanges, mercantile Dundee was on the up. The sense of well-being at the end of the century heightened with pride late in 1797 when news filtered through that the town's son Adam Duncan had defeated the Dutch fleet off Camperdown, a victory of sufficient magnitude to be celebrated with bells, bonfires and rejoicing across the country, but neglected by today's maritime histories in favour of subsequent events at Trafalgar.

During a visit in 1784, the great Methodist leader John Wesley noted, 'The spirit of improvement prevails in Dundee.' And, as the 1700s drew to a close, he concluded, 'We went to Perth, certainly the sweetest place in all North Britain, unless perhaps Dundee.'

6

1800 to 1850
BANKING ON LINEN

Dundee's population in 1800 was estimated at 23,000. By 1851 it had more than trebled to 79,000, half born outside its boundaries. It had become an eager, bustling town 'crowded with people'. It had also by then moved ahead of Hull as Britain's biggest importer of flax and overtaken Leeds to become the nation's leading linen producer. What happened? What transformed Provost Riddoch's couthy burgh into a dynamic manufacturing heavyweight in just half a century?

We need to visit an unassuming street bypassed in Dundee histories. This is Guthrie Street, where the Blackness Road swoops down to meet the city centre, an untidy cul-de-sac area bounded by the West Port, Marketgait and Lochee Road triangle, where redundant mill properties have been rediscovered and transformed into cavernous homes for ambitious small industries. What remains on the north side of Guthrie Street includes D. C. Thomson's West Ward printing works and the Prestige kitchen showroom. Down a metal manhole cover in the former, at No 19, lies the pond from the Scouring Burn which powered the first steam textiles engine in Dundee – the core of what was to become the world centre of linen and jute production. Its neighbour, the showroom, is housed in East Mill, once the most advanced linen factory in the world. There, during development in the 1970s, workmen found a flat-bottomed boat that had been tied up on the factory engine pond almost two centuries earlier. From such humble beginnings in the 1790s, spinning a couple of tons of flax a day into coarse brown linen, rose an unrivalled textiles industry that would soon boast the world's biggest linen factory in the Dens Works of Baxter Brothers.

The mechanisation pioneered by these merchant-manufacturers in Guthrie Street either side of 1800 removed hand-spinners and weavers from their rural cottage industry to the centralised production sites in the heart of Dundee – the beginnings of Juteopolis. Yet most visitors to today's city are not aware of the historic ground they are walking to reach Verdant Works jute museum around the corner, nor of the complex layers of industrial history they pass on their way to learning how this area later had the densest concentration of jute mills in the world.

In their pockets are the totems of our fast-moving technological world – mobile phones, Palm computers and iPods. These had a historical parallel. Entrepreneurial forebears harnessed successive technical advances to transform hand-processing into mechanical spinning: John Kay's Flying Shuttle of 1733 meant that broader cloth could be woven; James Hargreaves' Spinning Jenny in 1764 could spin eight threads at once; Richard Arkwright's prototype water-frame in 1769 allowed cotton to be spun for the first time, and the spinning mule, invented by Samuel Crompton in 1779, combined the moving carriage of the Jenny with the roller of Arkwright's water-frame to spin finer cloths. Yet progress in adapting flax fibres for mechanical spinning was much slower than for cotton – and Napoleon I of France offered one million francs to any inventor who could do it.

In 1787, however, John Kendrew and Thomas Porthouse of Darlington secured a patent for a machine to spin yarn from flax. In 1791 Edmund Cartwright began using power looms in a Manchester mill, which completed the mechanisation of the weaving process, and by the mid-decade, power machinery was to be found in a handful of ambitious mills across Britain spinning flax into linen cloth or thread.

The first ones in Dundee, at Guthrie Street and Bell Street in 1793, were powered by Boulton & Watt engines from Birmingham and had 'a preparing frame and two or three spinning frames, each driven by a blind man turning a crank'. The three-storey East Mill in Guthrie Street, a converted tannery, followed in 1799, and is considered by jute historian Mark Watson (1990) as 'one of the oldest surviving steam-driven mills in the world' and 'of immense archaeological value'. Here, the first manager William Brown recorded life in his diaries: of how the foreman played the violin as he walked up and down the factory floor on his supervisory duties – music while they worked for the mill's 103-strong, bleary-eyed staff on a twelve-hour day starting at 5.30 a.m. James Brown's Bell Mill followed in 1806, and its extraordinary fireproof construction became the template for new-build mills for the next twenty years – its advanced iron frame anticipating twentieth-century skyscrapers.

Few commercial experiments race away to instant success and so it was with Dundee's pioneering steam mills. All were forced to close or convert around 1810 when the Emperor of Russia blockaded the Baltic, severing supplies of the raw flax best suited to steam machinery and pushing up prices of home-grown flax to outrageous levels. Tay Street Mill was one of several advertised for public sale. It had a twelve-horsepower steam engine and eight spinning frames of thirty spindles each. David Cathro had put in machinery to the value of £8000 in 1809–10. The upset price in 1812 was just £4000. The Milnhouse steam mill in North Tay Street, with an 'engine on Watt and Boulton's principle', was another to close with heavy losses and be listed for sale. The building at 19 Guthrie Street became a flour mill.

Although Dundee still had many manual flax looms in its domestic weaving suburbs, the introduction of steam-powered spinning technology struck at the heart of handloom weaving. Word spread quickly that an unskilled boy could weave three and a half pieces of material on a power loom in the time a skilled weaver wove only one. Handloom weavers could not compete and faced wage cuts, if they could find work. Lancashire cotton mills fitted with engines were attacked in 1812 by Luddite handworkers who turned their anger against machinery that could put them out of work. In Dundee in 1816 inflated food prices led to riots in which six shops and houses were plundered – but the underlying cause of the anger was the meagre wages paid to weavers. Peter Carmichael, first manager of Baxter Works, recorded that hand weavers 'were ready to resist whatever seemed to them an encroachment on their trade'.

Relations with Russia restored, venture capitalists took advantage of Dundee's outstanding location for Baltic trade. Shipping records show regular connections to Archangel for flax from the growing areas north of Moscow, large imports from St Petersburg when the White Sea was frozen, and quantities of cheaper flax from Latvia and Estonia, shipped through Riga. A boom in building and converting linen mills capitalised on the demand for ships' canvas, uniforms, tents and hammocks during the Napoleonic Wars – with Baxter's, in a PR masterstroke, providing the sailcloth for Nelson's *Victory*. Baxter's manager, Peter Carmichael, usefully recorded the production process: 'The flax merchant made the importation of flax and hemp his business; the flax spinner bought the flax from him and, after getting it hackled [separating the fibres], span it by machinery into yarn; the manufacturer or household weaver bought the yarn from the spinner and had it woven in hand-looms into linen; then the linen merchant bought the cloth and, after having it bleached if necessary, found markets for it both at home and abroad.'

In 1821–2 alone, a dozen power mills were spun out across Dundee, benefiting from government linen bounty while at the same time negotiating a national banking crisis. Among them was the great Dens Works, begun by Baxter Brothers in 1821, which would grow rapidly over the following half century. During this period William Brown's diary describes an experimental period of night spinning at the East Mill. The novelty of night working seemed at first attractive: 'No mechanics are working, nor repairs and alterations going on – no improvements to schemes – no hecklers to attend – no flax or tow arriving – no yarn sending off – no warehouses open – no strangers calling – no materials to provide, such as coal, oil, tallow, and thousands others – no money to put away – no accounts to keep – no diet hours to interrupt business.'

Brown found, however, that while night spinning was profitable it was hopelessly problematic. Some hands never appeared for their shift. Others fell asleep. Linen was pilfered under cover of darkness. Machinery was badly maintained and lighting inadequate. He quickly concluded that, 'Night spinning should not be commenced again without great caution and consideration' and, 'In short, the business was everything but pleasure.'

Another fourteen new mills appeared between 1822 and 1834, the most impressive the spookily-shaped Coffin Mill in Brook Street, the second largest textiles factory in Scotland when constructed in 1828. The new mills had eaten up every spare area of ground near a water course and consumed 15,000 tons of flax a year. Dundee was on the cusp of irreversible physical and social change.

This astonishing expansion highlighted the limitations of the town's harbour. Mechanisation and the productivity it created required a large local workforce and the presence of a bigger and better port to handle incoming raw materials and the export of finished goods. Warehouses and weigh houses, wharves with steam cranes and customs rooms were required, and skeletal ships began to occupy timber launch stands. Tellingly, the new chief cargo of coastal vessels was coal to fuel the steam engines installed in the town. Increased supply and demand brought larger ships into port, necessitating the reclamation of land to build deep-water quays.

In 1815 a great procession from the Meadows led to the laying of the foundation stone of the new harbour negotiated in Provost Riddoch's final years in local government. It was badly needed. By 1822 the port boasted 158 vessels, and 1361 seamen. There were seven shipping companies. Exports of flax had risen from 1221 tons at the termination of government Napoleonic contracts in 1815, up to nearly 15,000 tons within ten years. By 1821, eight of every ten ships entering Dundee from foreign ports were vessels from the eastern Baltic. Vast crowds also gathered for the opening of Thomas Telford's King William IV Dock in 1825 and the Earl Grey Dock in 1834, developments which eased a situation described by the *Advertiser* as 'vessels being detained for weeks before they could get berths'.

The rush to prosperity had also harnessed advancing technology. The *Tay*, launched in Dundee in 1814, was one of the first six steam ships in the world. The *Union*, built in 1820, was the first to have a reversible gear, which earned its inventor James Carmichael a statue in Albert Square. With the new improvements in place, Dundee quietly overtook Hull as Britain's premier importer of Baltic flax. It had also outstripped Leeds, then with nineteen flax-spinning mills and 80,000 inhabitants, as Britain's leading manufacturer of linen.

Less is recorded of the markets for Dundee linen. Jackson's study of shipping (1991) showed that there was 'disdain' for British linen on the Continent, where people thought it inferior, or produced their own, or where protectionism was practised. Instead, the demand for linen lay with transatlantic colonies with which Dundee 'had no tradition of trade and for which she was imperfectly located'.

From around 1815, Canada was one of these markets, taking about a quarter of Dundee's exports. Ships conveyed large quantities of clothing for frontier settlements – although the *Psyche* in 1815 also carried a terrestrial globe and children's toys to Quebec. Settlement colonies in the United States developed into an even larger market for Dundee's manufacturing output. An average of a dozen ships a year sailed directly to New York in the 1820s and, until the speculators' 'bust' year of 1836, conveyed better linen for household use and coarser material for cotton bagging. Linen exports to New England rose astonishingly from 130,000 yards in 1815 to nine million yards in 1821. But by 1821 Dundee's business community had rediscovered another outlet for the town's product, one properly excised at customs but usually excised from town histories – the slave trade.

Firmly established in North America, trade moved south, resuming with the ports of New York and Charleston, South Carolina, after the American War of Independence and extending to the West Indies. Vast quantities of Dundee's linen was used to clothe slaves as manufacturers accessed the growing empire being carved out in the Americas. Ships began sailing directly to the slave capitals of Savannah, New Orleans, Mobile and Charleston, the major point of entry for Africans brought to America, with cargoes of cheap, coarse cloth to be stitched together in situ for the loose-fitting outer garments worn by slaves on plantations.

The yearly clothing of slaves included two coarse linen shirts, one pair of linen trousers and one jacket. The clothing was usually very rough and inadequate and dull in colour. Female slaves had dresses made from osnaburg, commonly called 'Negro cloth', which was the heavy coarse cotton made in Dundee and some other linen centres, and used in this country for sacking. Records of runaway slaves, which always gave detailed information about their clothing, provide some of the most telling evidence of the imported linen products they wore. In the *Virginia Gazette* in 1775, for example, Adam, aged twenty-three, ran away from Brandon Parish, Prince George County, while wearing 'Osnaburg shirt, Negro cotton jacket, Old blue cloth breeches and Cotton gambadoes'. When

Stephen, aged about twenty-one, escaped on New Year's Day 1775, he wore an osnaburg shirt, and 'carried off' [stole] two more osnaburg shirts. As Dundee was called upon to meet a strong demand for linen products, over a million yards was sent to Charleston alone in 1821.

Dundee was never a slave trading port like Bristol or Liverpool – and yet it developed a virtual monopoly in the supply of cheap, low-grade slave clothing. It was in a reduced sense similar to Glasgow during its exploitation of tobacco markets, which were based on the slave trade. Profiting from slavery remains an uncomfortable part of Dundee's history, and there are buildings in the city which were paid for by the profits of the trade, just as Glasgow has its tobacco mansions. It would be interesting if the city followed the recent move in Liverpool, where 'all streets, squares and public places named after those who were involved in promoting or profiteering from the slave trade' are to be renamed.

Worse, although Dundee had sanctioned the abolition of slavery in the 1780s, manufacturers had little enthusiasm for abolition and continued to exploit colonial slave markets until it was outlawed throughout the British Empire in 1833. Jackson notes that Dundee Chamber of Commerce refused to support abolition. The niche for cheap slave clothing was central to the town's economy. Emancipation would have threatened its manufacturing base. Faced by protest meetings, the publication of anti-slavery local pamphlets and the increased use of cotton in America's southern states, Dundee turned to the plantations of the Caribbean, exporting nearly four million yards to Jamaica, Haiti and San Domingo in the later 1820s. In one yearly quarter alone in 1831, 600,000 yards were shipped to Jamaica, 530,000 yards to Haiti and

570,000 yards to Brazil as the town continued to attract what a Dundee pamphlet of 1792 called 'the wealth derived from the horrible traffic' which 'spreads inconceivable anguish'.

In this pre-jute era of prosperity, improvements dominated the thinking of the town council. Ward Road was laid out and opened in 1803. Barrack Street, formerly Burial Wynd, followed in 1807, after burgesses complained that its name was 'doom laden' and unsuited to the forward-looking community. In 1810 the town's first purpose-built theatre opened in Castle Street: 'a capacious pit, three tiers of boxes, the seats stuffed and covered with beautiful scarlet cloth'. The site of the theatre is marked by a bust of Shakespeare high on the west side of the street, alluding to the possible but unlikely visit of the Bard with the Lawrence Fletcher touring company in 1601.

In 1824, a new police commission was formed to improve the policing of the burgh and that year the council petitioned central government for funds to provide for better paving, lighting and a prison, for which there was 'a great need'. Gas arrived in 1825 and the town was suddenly supplied with 'a cheap and beautiful light'. In 1826 construction began on the Dundee to Newtyle railway, ambitiously carrying an engine through a tunnel under the Law. The elegant Exchange Coffee House, known to many as Winter's the Printers, boasted 400 subscribers when it opened in 1828, each paying £1 a year to pass through its neo-classical columns and sit at tables provided by Trotter & Co, the pre-eminent cabinetmaker of Edinburgh. And by 1830, the growing wealth of the burgh was evident by the presence of seven independent banks, all eager to lend to new speculators, such as the young John Valentine, who launched his wood-block engraving business in 1825, later James Valentine and Sons, one of the largest mass-producers of picture postcards in the world.

The 1800s also brought Dundee's first proper newspaper, *The Dundee Weekly Advertiser*. The eight-page paper boasted a circulation of 600 and thumped out a reforming Liberal message to counteract the Tory *Glasgow Herald* and *Aberdeen Journal*, though it had to poach the *Journal*'s printer for its launch in January 1801. The *Advertiser*'s third and most famous early editor, Robert Rintoul, introduced the short leader articles on current political topics continued by *The Courier* to this day.

In many respects, the *Advertiser* was the outcome of the free-speech debates of the late 1700s and it was Rintoul, later the founding editor of *The Spectator*, who attracted the *Advertiser*'s first but not last libel suit, having upset Dundee's provost with criticism of his administration. The radicalism of one of Rintoul's cronies, William Lyon Mackenzie, later helped to shape Canada, his revolutionary role in the legislature commemorated by a plaque near the Old Steeple. Coincidentally, it was the brig *Psyche* in 1820 which took Mackenzie to his new home and future greatness.

On the home political front, the expanding town saw its first Member of Parliament George Kinloch take his seat in the House of Commons in 1832. Kinloch had been outlawed for sedition after leading a mob of 10,000 on Magdalen Green protesting against the Peterloo massacre of 1819. A dozen years is a long time in politics and after the necessary political upheaval his sentence was rescinded and he was despatched to Parliament with popular support. Reform Street was named after the 1832

Reform Act which took Kinloch to Westminster. Many radicals were disillusioned at the restrictive nature of the Act, which allowed only one in seven adult males to vote. Consequently not everybody was happy with the name of the new street. Some councillors proposed to call it Mortgage Place in allusion to the money borrowed to pay for it. The Alliance Trust, who have their headquarters in the street, and who presently manage funds worth £2.8 billion, would have relished playing footsie with the problem.

Dundee was on the move. It was a town where 'merchants, manufacturers, writers and shopkeepers' were building elegant homes to the east and west of the town centre, on the gentle slopes of the Law and on the opposite side of the river. Business, said the *Statistical Account* of 1833, was transacted chiefly before dinner, and evenings 'were often devoted to domestic enjoyment'. Dundee had, it concluded, 'a buoyant spirit of intelligence, enterprise, assiduous labour and successful speculation'. And still there was not a fibre of jute in sight.

For all the relentless development and profitable returns from linen, periodical downturns and multiplying social problems troubled the rapidly-urbanising community. Among concerns, ironically, was 'the impurity of the atmosphere arising from smoke of steam engines used in the manufactories'. The 'denseness' of the population in certain districts and a general lack of hygiene were also subjects of criticism. The provision of clean, drinkable water was a continuing problem and the Lady Well remained the town's principal water source. Not surprisingly, disease was seldom far away. A typhoid outbreak in 1819 involved 1264 cases and led to ninety-five deaths. The Dundee surgeon William Dick published an inquiry into the outbreak the following year and found 'some living in low cellars, noxious by their dampness, and without even a hole to admit either light or air, save by the door'. He added, 'I have found four or five of a family in holes not eight feet square, where two or three were lying sick in a corner.'

Diseases such as typhus, which affected the sickly and undernourished, spread quickly in the close confines of a mill. Cholera crossed society's class barriers and left many dead in 1832. Smallpox, which terrified everyone, stalked urban Dundee long after it faded in rural communities. While the population jumped by 30,000 in the twenty years between 1841 and 1861, only 568 new houses were built for the working classes. Tenemented properties were divided, then let, then sub-let, then filled six to a room. Small wonder that a new burial ground was badly needed, 'the present one being fearfully overcrowded'.

Working-age men jumped from this domestic frying pan headlong into the fat . . . or rather the blubber . . . of the better-paid whaling industry. Dundee whalers were dispatched to Arctic waters every spring bank holiday with the cheers of vast crowds speeding them on their way with oranges, red herrings and pennies thrown from shore to ship for luck by well-wishers. Only when the town's portside boiling yards had converted the catch of blubber on their return would bonus money be paid to the men – and depending on the success or otherwise of the voyage they might be in debt or they might have made a small fortune. Dundee, in common with other whaling ports, showed cyclical patterns of profit and loss. Speculators, too, were venturing into unmapped territory.

Huge numbers of whales were taken in the decades after 1800 and many thousands of seals were slaughtered for their skins and oil. Yet hunting whales and escaping ice remained a hazardous and dangerous enterprise, risky both for the financial backers in Dundee and for the masters and crews who annually faced severe Arctic conditions. Losses reached a peak in 1830 when, of the ninety-one British ships in Davis Strait, nineteen were lost and twenty-one returned to port 'clean', with no catch. Then, in the saddest episode in Dundee's whaling history, over seventy men were lost from two vessels in 1836, leaving 'one hundred fatherless bairns' in the town. The toll of such losses and the declining number of whales acted as a turning point in British Arctic whaling. From a peak of over 160 vessels in 1815, barely thirty sailed in 1840. Yields dropped, companies failed, boiling yards closed and men were paid off. London abandoned whaling in 1835 and Leith in 1840. The once-mighty Aberdeen fleet was cut to three vessels by 1839. Dundee was not immune from the recession. Three of the town's whaling companies were put up for sale in the 1840s, along with their ships and equipment. The industry was left hanging by a thread . . . a jute thread.

Miranda Seymour's masterful biography of *Frankenstein* author Mary Shelley (2000) suggests that Dundee's whaling trade gave Mary Godwin, as she was then, the inspiration for her scary novel. William Godwin of London had sent the sickly fourteen-year-old to stay with the Baxters of Broughty Ferry – of the linen dynasty – despatching his only daughter on the six-day voyage north on the appropriately named *Osnaburgh*. Mary remained in Dundee for much of 1812–14, enjoying the company of William Baxter's brood of artistic-leaning daughters and, among other leisurely pursuits, watching the comings and goings of whaling ships on the estuary. Seymour concluded, 'The story which encloses the tale of Victor Frankenstein and his scientific experiment is of an ambitious young man who sets off to find a new land beyond the North Pole, following the route taken by whaling vessels.'

Mary Shelley herself recalled in her preface to the 1831 edition of *Frankenstein* that the days in the comfortable house overlooking the Firth of Tay were, 'The eyry of freedom, and the pleasant region where I could commune with the creatures of my fancy.' She added, 'It was beneath the trees of the grounds belonging to our house, or on the bleak sides of the woodless mountains near, that my true compositions, the airy flights of my imagination, were born and fostered.' It does, therefore, seem that *Frankenstein* was shaped during her stay in Dundee. That her inspiration came from the whaling fleet is possible. There were terrible tragedies at the time – including the loss of the *Jane* off Broughty Ferry in 1809 and the *Rodney*, wrecked in Greenland in 1810. Her description of treeless mountains is said by Seymour to refer to the Law. The barren Sidlaw peaks of Balkello and Craigowl, north of the city, provide another intriguing possibility for the launch of the author's imaginary peregrination.

Far removed from the tragedy of Arctic losses, the heroic actions of another woman inspired the nation at this time. When Grace Darling helped to rescue men from the SS *Forfarshire*, which struck the Farne Islands in 1838 en route to Dundee, *The Times* gushed, 'Is there, in the whole field of history or of fiction, even one instance of female heroism to compare for one moment with this?' The Dundee ship's stern was swept away, carrying the captain, his wife and the cabin passengers to their deaths. A passing ship later picked up nine men in a lifeboat. The forward half of the vessel remained jammed and eleven survivors clambered on to the rocks. Two children were to die in their mother's arms before Grace Darling and her lighthouse-keeper father William could reach the survivors.

Seven of the nine saved by the Darlings were from Dundee. An unprecedented amount of publicity followed. Medals and money were gifted to her, artists queued up to paint her and day-trippers flocked to Longstone lighthouse in the hope of catching a glimpse of the heroine. Tragedy followed tragedy. Grace Darling died of tuberculosis in 1842, just four years after the rescue. She was only twenty-five.

That year, 1842, could have seen Robert Allison proudly showing his wife Dundee's new Customs House, where he had just been appointed manager. He could have boasted to her that it was the largest in the country, and had captured architectural fashion with its mighty Ionic columns. He could have described its magnificent chambers for the Harbour Board. He could have mentioned the 318 vessels now using Dundee as their home port, exactly double the number listed twenty years earlier. It was not to be. Mrs Allison with her son and grandson were among the cabin passenger victims of the *Forfarshire*.

Customs House was one of several impressive buildings and new streets reflecting the growing prosperity of textile and shipping manufacturers in this phase of the industrial revolution. Panmure Street was laid out, Bell Street extended and St Andrew's Cathedral finished, all in 1839 – the end of a decade in which Dundee experienced an extraordinary forty per cent leap in population.

Other new churches were hurriedly constructed after the religious schism of 1843 – though a disastrous fire two years earlier had left venerable St Mary's a smoking ruin. The catalogue of its library of medieval books was reputedly thrown from a window of the blazing building, picked up by a bystander and taken to Australia during the gold rush of the 1850s, before being returned in 1910. And, with the coming of the railways, just a year or two after George Stephenson's Stockton-to-Darlington locomotive had chugged into history, Broughty Ferry was greatly extended on a gridiron system. Dundee's middle classes were no longer anchored to town-centre homes. And when Queen Victoria passed under the hurriedly-constructed Royal Arch on her visit to Dundee in September 1844 she must have been mightily impressed with the town's new-found importance and limitless ambition – and faintly amused when the city's theatrical art-collecting MP George Duncan upstaged the entire town council by appearing in a bizarre courtly costume.

One wonders whether the young queen also called into the printer's shop in Castle Street to tell the proprietor James Chalmers how taken she was with her portrait on the new penny and twopenny stamps, the world's first. Chalmers (1782–1853) was an Arbroath-born weaver who moved to Dundee in 1809 to start a printing business. He had first suggested the adhesive postage stamp in 1834. In 1839, the public was asked to submit suggestions for a pre-paid penny post system to a parliamentary committee considering Rowland Hill's proposals for postal service reforms. Chalmers sent in the designs and costs for a uniform penny post system, produced on his presses in Castle Street, while Hill submitted a plan for the use of adhesive printed wrappers. Both wrappers

Mars Training Ship, 1929

Chimneys from Law Hill, 1930

Queue outside book store, c1934

Jessie Jordan, 1938

Housewives' protest, 1948

Workers leaving Camperdown
Works, 1950

Gateway to Bowbridge Works,
1951

City Square, Coronation celebrations, 1953

Building Fintry scheme, 1956

Dundee's last tram, 1956

Snowballing at Baxter Park, 1958

Pylons in Balgowan Avenue,
Kirkton, 1958

Eagle Jute Mills, c1960

Interior of Hamilton Carhartt Ltd, 1961

Children in Findale Street, Fintry, 1963

Marks and Spencer, c1964

Cars emerging from Camperdown Park, 1964

Maxwelltown multi-storey flats, 1967

Tower block, Belmont Hall, 1967

Women in Dens Road Market, 1971

Bytom ship launch, Caledon Yard, 1979

Derelict tenement, Graham Place, 1984

Demolition of mill, Dens Road, 1984

Amstrad printer assembly, Timex Ltd, 1986

and the famous Penny Black stamp were introduced in 1840, but it was Hill, as the man responsible for implementing the Penny Postage Bill of 1839, who was knighted by a grateful sovereign and who received a public testimonial of £15,000.

It was left to the Penny Black-affronted town council to offer Chalmers public recognition for his efforts – and for frustrated philatelists from that day to this to argue the precedence of his discoveries over that of the 'impostor' Hill. Chalmers certainly produced the first specimens for stamps, using one on a trial letter on which he applied a black postmark *Dundee, October 7, 1839*. He should also receive credit for using the town name and date to cancel stamps, which has since become the integral feature of every postal service in the world. And when he sent a copy of one of his twopenny stamps to the secretary of the General Post Office in 1839, it was the first time an envelope bearing an adhesive stamp had passed through the mails. James Chalmers is buried in the Howff graveyard, opposite the city's main post office. Hill was interred in Westminster Abbey.

Chalmers also published the *Dundee Directory* of 1829–30, a slim volume 112 pages in length. I have been shown, from a private collection, a larger, more detailed manuscript version of the printed directory, in which Chalmers provides a snapshot of his adopted town in beautiful copperplate writing. He estimates its population at 40,000, some 10,000 greater than the figure provided in the 1821 Census. Among occupations he lists nine auctioneers and twenty-six doctors and surgeons. There are as many solicitors as teachers. He provides details of six banks in the town. He discusses trade with the West Indies, Greenland and America and, of course, the Baltic seaports. He lists cabin passage to London from Dundee at £3. 3 shillings, with passage in 'steerage' at half that amount.

Chalmers' manuscript provides a wonderful flavour of the developing town, but does not anticipate the transition from linen to jute that was just around the corner. It is usually stated that demand caused by the Crimean War (1853–6) and the American Civil War (1861–5) – and even the 1851 Australian gold rush with its 'towns' of tents – accelerated jute production in Dundee. They were certainly factors which had a stimulating effect on its development, as did the threat of interruption to flax supplies, and the happy coincidence of whale oil's lubricating effect on raw jute. There was also periodic slackness in the linen trade, which encouraged manufacturers to experiment with jute fibres, notably after the linen price slump of 1836 in which 'in one week thousands of handlooms were silenced'.

But Mark Watson hit the nail firmly on the head when he concluded that the price of jute was key to the textiles revolution in Dundee. In 1834, for example, raw jute was £12 a ton while Baltic flax averaged around £50. Watson (1990) noted, 'Over the next 40 years jute fluctuated between £15 and £30, always less than half the price of flax.' So the attraction of jute – which could be used like other textiles for a variety of products – was obvious. It was the cheaper option, and the smarter one for the town's cohort of ever-watchful speculators.

Most certainly the city's linen industry did not disappear overnight, but co-existed with jute in the manner that handlooms and powerlooms shared production in the early 1800s. In fact, one of Dundee's biggest and most influential employers, Baxter Brothers of Dens Works, remained loyal to linen. But mill after mill was converted for the preparatory and spinning stages of the new fibre as the transfer to jute forged ahead. The first direct shipment of jute from Calcutta was carried aboard the *Selma* in April 1840. Her master, Captain Luckie, was awarded the Freedom of Dundee for successfully conveying 100 bales on this historic passage. As to where raw jute was first spun mechanically in Dundee, Watson and others suggest the now-demolished Chapelshade Mill in Bell Street. I would place this on the site of the main entrance to Abertay University, formerly Dundee Technical Institute. It was here, coincidentally, that historic machinery from the jute era was mothballed in preparation for the time when the city would be able to show its staple industry in a better light – today's Verdant Works museum.

At the start of the 1800s the Dens and Scouring Burns could not satisfy the demands of water-driven flax mills, thereby accelerating the introduction of Dundee's prototype steam-power factories in Guthrie Street and elsewhere. Yet curiously, the dozens of steam-driven mills to emerge in the early 1800s were converted or constructed around these traditional watercourses. This was about to change. Dundee was on the verge of expanding its boundaries and industrial base beyond all recognition. It already boasted over forty spinning mills, eight power loom factories, and over sixty handloom factories, employing 11,000 people in linen manufacture. That was nothing compared to the coronation and mighty reign of King Jute.

7

1850 to 1900

KING JUTE: A MIGHTY MONARCH

Jute is the first monolith of the 'jute, jam and journalism' triumvirate that indelibly placed Dundee on the long line of maps begun by Matthew Paris in 1250. Yet one important element escapes Verdant Works – Dundee's former European Industrial Museum of the Year, which tells the industry's story. Missing are the endless rows of working people, the women, men and children who made the bobbins fly and the mills bustle. At its peak, jute spinning and weaving employed 40,000 people in the city's 125 mills, an almost inconceivable tally of toil. The names of the mills – Manhattan Works, Craigie Works, Caldrum Works, Ashton Works, Bowbridge Works, Tay Works, Dura Works – are being forgotten with every passing generation. Yet walk along any Dundee street, talk to the elderly, and unshakeable familial links will be rapidly established to the ebb and flow of this one-time lifeblood industry.

How can we put into context the unique industrialisation and urbanisation which took place in the second half of nineteenth-century Dundee? Think of all the employees at NCR today, add those at Michelin and D. C. Thomson, and everyone in call-centre jobs in the city. The total would scarcely match the number employed in just one factory when jute powered Dundee in its manufacturing heyday.

The Camperdown Works at Lochee employed 6000 at its peak and was the largest textiles factory in Europe. The works covered twenty-five acres and was dominated by a 280-foot chimney made from 1,000,001 bricks. It was the finest lum in Scotland, and it belched out the residue of the High Mill, 'the greatest Victorian textile mill in Scotland'. Camperdown was so big it had its own railway station. Look at today's huge car park, mill housing, supermarket, bowling alley, former cinema and restaurants, landscaping north, south, east and west: this was once all a monolithic jute-manufacturing complex which gave Lochee a unique character and standing in the town. Call it a suburb, call it the people's republic, but Lochee has remained 'independent' of Dundee ever since. Elsewhere, the monumental Tay Works, stretching along Marketgait, empire of the mighty Gilroy Brothers, was the largest textile mill in Britain when completed in 1865. Bowbridge Works, 'home' to 3000 hands, featured a dining room and an amusement hall, and the last of the great mills, James Caird's Ashton Works in Hawkhill, boasted a steam-driven drive shaft which, turned on its end, would have lorded it over the Law.

Between 1851 and 1881 Dundee's population grew from 79,000 to 140,000 – rising at a rate double that of Scotland as a whole. But what made the town really different was that two-thirds of its employed population worked in manufacturing industries, compared to a third in Aberdeen and Edinburgh and a half in Glasgow. And one out of every two was a servant of what the *Advertiser* christened King Jute. Edinburgh had just one in a hundred in textiles. With whaling oiling the wheels of jute preparation, engineers supporting the trade with brilliant Heath Robinsonesque adaptations, and an experienced if reluctant labour force, the jute industry was almost entirely located in the Dundee district. No other major British industry, not even the extensive Lancashire cotton industry, was concentrated in such a small area. Eight major employers each boasted over 1500 employees by the 1860s, and between 1870 and 1874 alone the number of spindles and looms doubled as the linen-to-jute revolution continued during this golden age of mill building.

While linen once provided the sailcloth for British shipping, tenting for Europe's armies and clothing for Afro-Caribbean slaves, coarse, brittle jute was used mostly for packing purposes, made into sacks or wrapping materials for grain, wool or fertilisers, or for mailbags. In times of war it was used to make sandbags, military webbing, tents and tarpaulins. In the food industries it was adopted for sugar sacks and for packing Danish bacon. Important later uses included furniture upholstery and backing for tufted carpet and linoleum. Jute was in demand – and the town became the major producer in the world.

If jute made Victorian Dundee different, what made it unique in Britain was the reliance on women to make it profitable. For fifty years, Dundee was a single-industry women's town. Between the ages of twenty and forty, there were almost three women to every two men in the city – typically some 10,000–15,000 more of them. A higher proportion of women worked in Dundee than in other Scottish cities – and fifteen per cent more than in Scotland as a whole. And Dundonian women and girls were engaged in work very different from their contemporaries in comparable cities. Three of every four linen and jute employees, 30,000 out of 40,000, were women and girls. Moreover, the convenient absence of a marriage bar in the industry meant more married women worked in Dundee than in any other city, a dimension that continued until well into the twentieth century. The automatic escape from work through marriage was largely irrelevant in Dundee.

This made Dundee an extraordinary place in which to live. Women were not at home during the day, but often their men were. Women frequently had no time to make as much as a sandwich . . . but they were the breadwinners. So wives, mothers, widows and daughters did not conform to the female role. Instead their menfolk were the infamous 'kettle boilers' of Dundee, the 'loafers' left at home to mind the bairns. They felt worthless and humiliated, lounged about the house, or stood sullenly at street corners waiting for the pubs to open. And this unique swapping of economic roles gave the town a dynamic shared with no other. No wonder Dundee men, under-size and underage, rushed to the recruiting sergeant at the approach of war.

Dundee was a lop-sided city in more ways than the gender division of labour. There was little alternative work outside the mills, other than manual jobs in labour-intensive foundries, threadworks, tanneries and breweries. The middle classes simply did not exist and consequently there was little alternative housing. The super-rich had mansions in West Ferry which, along with Bowden in Manchester, home of the cotton barons, was one of the wealthiest residential areas in Britain. The working classes had their tenements, which offered only spirit-sapping overcrowding and permanent stench. In the congested area known as Blue Mountains in the Hawkhill, 1600 people lived in an area the size of a couple of football pitches. Between Lochee Road and the

Hawkhill was the greatest concentration of mills and with them 'miserable unwholesome dwellings'. The city centre was, as the jurist Lord Cockburn famously characterised it in 1852, 'a sink of atrocity which no moral flushing seems capable of cleansing'. One wonders whether the town's seething, seamy backstreets provided the fog, smoke, soot and filth that inspired Charles Dickens when he visited Dundee to open the Kinnaird Hall in 1858.

Into this Dickensian scene trudged unemployed rural folk seeking waged work. Those who failed, or who failed to settle, turned to opportunities elsewhere. From 1850 the *Advertiser* promised cheap passage to America and a new beginning that every schoolboy knew had provided prosperity for Protestant pioneers of the New World. A resigned, go-for-it attitude must have stirred the adult jobless – just as stowing away on a whaler was an attractive alternative to young boys faced with a bleak future as half-timers in the low mill.

Clippers – such as the Dundee-built *Maulesden*, which carried emigrants from Glasgow to Queensland in a record sixty-nine days – lined the wharves alongside whalers and convict ships. From 1869, the mariners on these sleek vessels could look out in the estuary at the ungainly sight of the *Mars* training ship. 'Ye'll get sent tae the *Mars*,' was a familiar parental threat to many a wayward Dundee lad. McGill (1995) showed that the moored former warship provided a home for boys who were destitute or abandoned, rather than one for those with a criminal record. Another finding was that the number of boys sent to the *Mars* from Glasgow greatly exceeded the number of Dundonians. There were also large contingents from London – which led to hilarious assaults on the hitherto impregnable Dundee dialect. One oddity was that 'threats' to be sent to the *Mars* were used by parents as recently as the 1980s, half a century after the floating 'borstal' had been towed to Inverkeithing and scrapped.

Money also flowed out of the city during this period of accelerated industrialisation. Cash-rich manufacturers poured profits into North American speculative schemes – cattle ranching in Texas, copper mining in Arizona, a railroad in Oregon. Although this economic development was financial, and thus less visible than the belching chimney smoke signalling the town's manufacturing credentials, some £275 million in today's values was spent on 'ranching mania' and other overseas investment between 1873 and 1883 alone. In the rush to take advantage of overseas opportunities, Dundee magnates effectively invented investment trusts as vehicles for surplus profits – but shareholders in Dundee often ended up with certificates as worthless as a losing lottery ticket.

Taking account of this speculative spending, local histories usually claim that jute profits were seldom ploughed back into the industry or used to address the problems of the working-class poor. It is short-sighted and simplistic, however, to emphasise the gulf between the minority rich and majority poor solely by contrasting their domestic situations. From his house in Roseangle, for example, James Caird sprinkled his massive fortune on charitable causes across his native city and beyond. Caird reached for his chequebook time and time again, but is most famous for the hall that bears his name, into which he sunk £100,000 (about £7 million today). When it was completed he opened the hall by pressing an electrical connection beneath the world's second-largest emerald, now in the Lord Provost's chain. Close to his beloved Ashton jute works in Hawkhill, the tall, greying, bearded Caird built a cancer hospital and a women's hospital, acquired rare Egyptian relics for Dundee Museum, bought Caird Park and the Caird Rest Home for the city, and left money after his death in 1916 for the purchase of Camperdown Park. He sent Shackleton on his way to the Antarctic with a sum equivalent to £1.7 million, built an insect house at London Zoo and provided ambulances for the Balkan wars.

If his sister could not equal his showy paternalism, her generosity matched his own. Gifts during Mrs Marryat's lifetime included £10,000 to clear Dundee Royal Infirmary's debts, £55,000 to purchase Belmont Castle, £75,000 to finish and equip the Caird and Marryat Halls, and £25,000 for equipment at Dundee Royal Infirmary. The Caird bequests amounted to around £1 million, worth today about £75 million, and ensured the family name immortality in their native city.

Elsewhere, industrialists combined privately to fund the Albert Institute in 1876, the largest memorial to Queen Victoria's late husband outside London. Known as the McManus Galleries since a restoration project in 1983, the galleries and museum now housed in the premises should perhaps use the current refurbishment as an opportune time to return the majestic Sir George Gilbert Scott building to its original name. The first Tay Bridge was supported financially by linen and jute manufacturers, while the best-known of individual legacies is the art collection bequeathed by James Orchar to the people of Broughty Ferry and controversially ceded to the McManus Galleries.

Thanks to the city's superbly green-fingered gardeners, the lungs of inner-city Dundee – Caird Park, Lochee Park,

Baxter Park, Dudhope Park, Dawson Park and Balgay Park – have always been in better shape than those of the people using them. These, too, were mostly the legacy of moneyed textile employers. The best of them, Baxter Park – one of only three parks laid out by the celebrated landscape designer Sir Joseph Paxton, and a rare example of an urban formal park – was the gift to the city of the linen manufacturer Sir David Baxter. Some 60,000 people witnessed its opening in 1863, when a holiday was declared, fireworks crackled and medals were struck. How splendid that lottery funding has helped to return it to its purpose.

Balgay Park, opened in 1871, has Britain's only municipal public observatory, a gift to the city by the jute manufacturer John Mills. Lochee Park was a gift in 1891 from the Cox Brothers of Camperdown jute works. The brothers bequeathed it principally for the 'working people of Lochee' and they exercised ownership by cutting down its trees for fuel during a lock-out. Dawson Park was the gift of William Dawson, a director of George Morton, wine and spirits merchants, and Caird Park, at 270 acres one of Scotland's largest urban parks, was one of Sir James Caird's many gifts. Dudhope Park, to the north of the city centre, was purchased by the town, as was the Law, bought for £4000 in 1878, while the old common ground of Magdalen Green dates to medieval times.

If jute manufacturers were slow to influence the domestic situation of employees directly through the provision of better working conditions and housing, they were prone to showing off their wealth not only on the jute palaces in which they lived, but on the mills and factories they operated. Extravagant architectural flourishes and magnificent iron-work, unrivalled in Scotland, captured their pride. A. & S. Hendry's Victoria Road finishing mill boasted an opulent marble staircase, Lawside Works an Italianate cupola, Camperdown polychrome brickwork and its fantastic chimney, Tay Works magnificent obelisks and pediments; even the Coffin Mill had a trendy flat-capped tower. The most grandiose flourish was the exotic camel and rider, modelled on Lawrence of Arabia, which eventually topped the gate of Gilroy Brothers' Bowbridge Works. Only after manufacturers had ceded control of the industry to Indian competition and profit-trimming had begun in the 1880s did the trend change to pragmatic, shed-style mills.

Newspapers played a role in attracting inward migration as well as encouraging emigration. Subtle adverts placed by jute manufacturers during the Irish potato famine tempted impoverished Irish workers to come to Dundee. Scotland was a tried and tested alternative for the Irish, as it is today for eastern Europeans. It was easy to get passage and work was waiting, particularly seasonal employment in harvesting, potato-picking and labouring. But Dundee had a specific requirement – feeding its worker-hungry textiles trade. In 1791, the Roman Catholic chapel had a congregation 'of just eight souls' in a population of around 20,000. By 1830 there were 2000 Irish in the town. By 1861, 15,000 Irish contributed to a total population of 90,000; in other words, one in six of Dundee's population was Irish-born, settling close to mills and factories, forming priest-controlled communities which resonate today in suburbs such as Dens Road and Lochee. Anti-Irish and anti-Catholic criticism followed. They were accused of taking local jobs and tempting mill owners to impose lower wages. They were also libelled in print, blamed for importing disease and for being politically disruptive. Anti-Irish anger was even channelled into boxing matches on top of the Law. Today, some 2000 young Irish people add a welcome dash of chatty energy to the city's student mix and do so without a hint of the suspicions of old.

Coping with a mushrooming population which saw a modest burgh town of 23,000 in 1800 transform into a vibrant industrial city of 161,000 by 1900, meant families squashing into squalid city-centre slums. The resulting social problems often prompted political mobilisation or militancy. Between 1870 and 1880 there were forty-six strikes within Dundee's jute and linen industries alone, accompanying a period of erratic wage movement. In 1875, 12,000 operatives from twenty-nine different works were out. In 1893, 15,000 workers walked out over a threatened reduction in wages. In 1895, 18,000 went on strike and a further 10,000 were thrown idle. In 1899, over 35,000 were locked out – an extraordinary figure in today's benign industrial relations climate.

Organisation to effect change was slow and when it came it was led by men. The Revd Henry Williamson, who coerced the hands into Scotland's first women's union in 1885, recorded that the majority of mill workers were unwilling at first to participate in union affairs. Although there was a spirit in the girls 'to fight for their rights' . . . 'not one could I persuade to accept office on the committee'. To an outsider, they were loud-voiced lassies with the light of battle in their defiant eyes, but jute girls had their own characteristics and unwritten codes of behaviour. While it was bordering on the hopelessly ambitious for public lectures to be arranged to instil in them appropriate behaviour and moral correctness, it was also wrong to tar them with one brush, as the able jute historian William Walker did: 'The millgirls were the despair of reformers and an embarrassment to employers and workers alike.' The *Dundee Advertiser*, with untypical bravado, added, 'Below the surf of industrious, respectable factory workers ebb and surge the flotsam and jetsam of the street – the millworkers.'

Sure, the word 'girlstrous' could have been invented for them, but it is both astonishing and insulting that the vociferous tradition of Victorian jute workers was used as a template to criticise women strikers at Timex in the 1990s. 'Witches of Dundee' *The Times* called them in 1993, while the *Observer* in June that year unhelpfully contributed, 'Dundee women are like no other'. In recent years, the radical history of women jute workers has also been 'blamed' for Dundee's teenage pregnancy epidemic, free-and-easy sex – and even rising rates of shoplifting.

While the Dundee newspapers were always happy to confirm unruly behaviour among poor jute girls, it was also the case that their wages were often little worse than those in other occupations. Dundee's weavers, who formed almost one third of all female textile workers, were paid up to £1 per week in 1890, worth about £75 today, when 'the low level of subsistence was just under 10 shillings', or half that amount. Fifteen years later, the nationally agreed wage for women war munitions workers still stood at £1. While some 800 youths under twenty were 'turned adrift' from jute mills every year, the welfare pioneer Mary Lily Walker noted, 'The jute industry relies mainly on the labour of women, girls and lads. For the latter it is more or less a blind alley occupation, but for women and girls it offers steady employment and in many departments good wages.'

In fact, the large reservoir of single working women in Dundee presented unique economic opportunities. Mary Lily Walker counted 10,000 more women than men between the ages of twenty and forty during data collection in 1904. And for these women, early marriages were not common. Towards the end of the century only one in five of 25,000 working females was married, which left the adult single women among the 20,000 waged females potentially economically independent. These jute women possessed far greater purchasing power than had been imagined to date. Moreover, in enjoying economic opportunity, they were free to exert a powerful influence on the general prosperity of the town and to some extent on its political direction. This is important. Rather than being economically destitute, as they are painted in so many histories, Dundee's infamous mill girls were not dependent on male goodwill for money as they would have been in more typical domestic situations, but often remained in control of their economic destinies with the independent spending power of steady and relatively remunerative employment.

What appears to have happened in Dundee is that many working girls and young women departed from the family unit as soon as they were earning enough and had plucked up courage to leave. Walker found that, 'It is a frequent complaint that young girls leave home when they earn good money, simply from the love of independence.' Thus they were by no means 'flotsam and jetsam'. They shared homes with sisters or companions, or they set up single homes, prudently and with a honed degree of management. This is why Dundee Women Citizens' Association persuaded the Robert Fleming trustees of the urgent need to build housing for single working women near Clepington Road.

By evading the situation of living in a family home – or not – female spinners and weavers had ample opportunity to engage in sexual activity. In the early years of the twentieth century, Dundee held the unenviable title for the highest number of illegitimate births in Scotland – almost one in every eight – as it does today for teenage pregnancies and for abortions. The town also had worryingly high rates of infant mortality – perhaps unsurprising, since some girls had babies virtually where they stood in the mill, and carried on working, almost more fearful of losing their job than they were of losing their child. In 1904, Dundee Social Union enumerated thirty-seven children who had died as a result of smothering – or 'overlaying' – in bedclothes. Such statistics led jute historian William Walker to make a controversial assertion that mothers in Dundee practised infanticide. Contemporary evidence tends to dilute Walker's argument, however. In June 1898, Elizabeth Martin of Watson's Lane appeared at Dundee Police Court on a charge which stated that she had 'while in a state of intoxication, lain in such a fashion on the body of her child, William, aged 17 days, as to prevent it breathing, with the result that the infant died'. Sheriff Campbell Smith pointed out that the death rate of infants was very high in the town, and that a great part of it was due to 'the smothering by drunken mothers'. Martin pleaded guilty to the lesser charge of neglect and was sentenced to thirty days in prison, but Sheriff Smith warned 'the drunken mothers of Dundee' that he would not be so lenient in the future.

Smith's emphasis on drunken mothers is probably an accurate social snapshot. At times more women than men were charged with drunkenness in Victorian Dundee and premature child death may have been the unfortunate outcome of such conduct. The notion that parents in cramped domestic confines suffocated their children by rolling on top of them while drunk is supported by the fact that just under half of these incidents occurred between Saturday night and Sunday morning. While Dundee Social Union investigators found that Dundee headed the list of fifteen principal towns in Scotland, with an infant mortality rate of 174 per 1000, authorities were satisfied that none of the children had been murdered for insurance money – noting that pay-outs for such deaths were relatively insignificant. And in 1904 the local Medical Officer for Health attributed the high levels of infant death to 'exceptional industrial conditions', with no criminality stated. In any case, such social events were often soaked up in the greater monarchy that was King Jute.

The second half of the nineteenth century continued to see massive imports of jute feed the town's staple industry – vessels devoted to the trade, one aptly called *Juteopolis*, took 100 days to sail from India. But with the decision to build factories in Calcutta, near an important source of the raw material, the beginning of the end for local trade was signalled. Dundee would be overtaken by the Indian city as the world centre of jute production and eventually its manufacture would be displaced from Scotland altogether. Much of the machinery and expertise used in the Indian trade came from the parent city, however, so that while construction of integrated spinning-weaving-finishing mills in Calcutta quickened, much of the wealth created continued to flow back to notable addresses in Broughty Ferry.

For those who decided to look elsewhere for work, it was common knowledge that men in the whaling trade could earn smaller fortunes. This took hopefuls to the harbourside whaling company offices to attempt to sign on for a season in the Arctic. It was no deterrent that thirty Dundee whaling ships already lay in an icy Arctic grave.

Dundee whaling crews lived with the ever-present prospect of insufferable cold, danger, deprivation and death. A harpooned whale could upset a flimsy whaleboat, dumping men into freezing water that killed them in seconds, but the greatest fear was being imprisoned in ice. Ships 'beset' offered only a terrible ordeal, leaving sailors stranded in an unknown land with few survival skills. Many men lost limbs from frostbite or faced the 'death monster' scurvy. James McIntosh of the *Chieftain* watched four comrades drink seawater in his stranded open boat and die one by one, insane. Left to his loneliness, he ate his hat and survived, but had both frostbitten legs removed on his return to Dundee in 1884. Journals written by numbed fingers tell of the barely living requisitioning the clothes of those who died in front of them. The frail wooden ships, too, paid a high price for their boldness in northern latitudes. Almost every year a ship failed to return to Dundee, squeezed and sunk under the ice-pack pressure of the Arctic whaling grounds.

Captains and crews took themselves to these limits of human endurance in order to reap the enormous profits of the catch. Arctic whaling was a means to acquire wealth, and for the participants it was often as profitable as it was dangerous, a journey of exhilaration, a life of adventure. Whaling anticipated the wealth of the North Sea era of oil and gas and of industrial plastics. Whale oil, the product of blubber, lit up British cities, lubricated the Industrial Revolution, provided the soap to wash off factory grime and smoothed the process of jute production in Dundee. Whalebone, washed and dried until tough and flexible, was used to make carriage springs, walking canes, whips, brushes, brooms, umbrella ribs and fishing rods. Most of all, whalebone was used for women's hooped skirts and the stiffening in corsets and other tight-laced undergarments, where great strength and lightness were required. At the Dundee quayside it changed hands for up to £3000 a ton as the expanding Victorian middle classes demanded waist-tightening undergarments.

So the men who signed articles in the whale company offices around Dundee's docks could earn more in one Arctic season than in five years in the jute mills. Mirroring the pioneers of the town's power mills, owners and crews were ever willing to speculate to accumulate – only in whaling, everyone from the captain to the ship's apprentice received a share of the profits.

Exhausted stocks and the loss of dozens of vessels in the 1830s had signalled the end of whaling in ports across the country. But in Dundee a timely restoration of fortunes returned through the decision to introduce steam power to the fleet in 1860. As it was with textiles, steam propulsion offered the whalers many advantages. It provided speed, ice-breaking capabilities, and safety in being able to press forward or to retreat cautiously. With the wooden-hulled steam fleet hastily constructed in the town by Alexander Stephen & Co, Dundee stole an advantage over Peterhead and other whaling centres, which had tried and failed with iron hulls. The city pursued steam power relentlessly and soon boasted the most powerful whaling fleet in the world. This encouraged whaling masters to push towards new horizons in the Arctic. What did not change was that the hunt for profit meant ships could be tempted to dally too long in unexplored seas or in changeable weather. Thus the industry remained as risky a venture as it had always been – and more Dundee whalers went to the bottom in the 'safe' era of steam than in the age of sail.

Dundee's whaling industry fell away from the 1870s as Right whales were hunted to the verge of extinction for quick returns in conditions that became increasingly arduous. Catches diminished in quantity and quality and ships lost were not replaced. Diversification attempts – longer voyages, exploitation of new areas, overwintering and especially Dundee's historic Antarctic expedition of 1892 – all proved fruitless in terms of the traditional whaling practices the port employed. As the whaling fleet faded into a chapter in Dundee's story, the crews of the *Active, Eclipse, Narwhal, Aurora, Snowdrop, Polar Star* and *Resolute*, and masters such as Captain Adams, Captain Milne, Captain Guy and Captain Yule, passed on traditions of mince and tatties, Scottish reels and porridge for breakfast to native Greenlanders. Less welcome were the guns and tobacco introduced by whalermen which are responsible today, say researchers, for ill health, violence and high suicide rates among Inuit populations.

The 1870s were important for reasons closer to home. Demand for textile products during the Franco-Prussian War of 1870–1 boosted profits. Increased prosperity, along with the implementation of the 1871 Improvement Act, spurred substantial physical change across the town. It brought the clearance of slum areas and the creation of new buildings and mills. Piped water became available, ending years of inadequate supplies. A municipal library was opened in 1870, a new museum in 1873 and four new schools followed the creation of school boards in

1872. Thoroughfares were widened or extended and dozens of new streets planned. Driven by manufacturing prosperity, the town extended up the hills behind the centre and along the shores. Yet there was never a determined design strategy, more an architectural anarchy. Dundee Royal Infirmary, built in 1855, was a grand neo-Tudor pile, while the Royal Exchange in Albert Square, finished a year later, was Flemish Gothic, emulating medieval architecture. In contrast, the courthouse, completed in Bell Street, followed the boldly-porticoed Grecian lines of the earlier Exchange Coffee House and Customs House. Morgan Academy (1868) was pseudo-French Gothic with a hint of Scots Baronial; the 1876 banking palace in Murraygate, lately vacated by the Clydesdale Bank, was Graeco-Italian, and the Queen's Hotel (1878), built in 12th-century French-Gothic style, has been aptly described as 'rumbustious' by Walker (1977). Topping them all was The Vine, an exceptional Egypto-Greek, Regency-style villa in Magdalen Yard Road, built for the celebrity MP George Duncan by the architect responsible for the A. K. Bell Library in Perth.

But the work that really kept the town builders busy in the second half of the nineteenth century was the hurried construction of cheap tenements for textile workers. In the decade 1871–80 alone, nearly 10,000 working-class houses were crammed close to spinning mills and factories, giving hands every encouragement to clock in on time for their non-stop, twelve-hour day.

This developing decade was brought down to earth with the disastrous collapse of the Tay Bridge in December 1879. The bridge took six arduous years to build and one tragic night to fall down. A supposed seventy-five lives were lost when a central section collapsed during an exceptional December storm, taking a Dundee-bound train and six carriages with it. Numerous theories have been put forward as to why the disaster happened. These range from high winds, to derailment, to structural weaknesses and flaws in the bridge. The collapse has also been attributed to bad workmanship, poor inspection and cost-cutting. The most recent study, by metallurgists at the Open University, concluded that many cast-iron 'lugs' or fixings, designed to hold the bracing bars for each column supporting the bridge, were broken or missing. The steady deterioration of the lugs on the high girders, coupled with high winds and the vibration of the train, probably caused the bridge to topple.

When completed in the summer of 1878, the Tay Bridge was not only the longest bridge in the world, it was hailed as a marvel of Victorian engineering. Its designer Thomas Bouch even rowed US President Ulysses Grant into the river to trumpet its brilliance prior to receiving the Freedom of Dundee. His reputation ruined, Bouch died a broken man. The stumps that survive today are responsible for the nervous gapes from present-day passengers crossing Sir William Arrol's no-nonsense successor structure of 1886. Their thoughts inevitably turn to that night's awful storm and the watery grave which faced terror-struck passengers like Margaret Kinnear, who was only seventeen when she died. Kinnear's black straw hat was found at Broughty Ferry two weeks after the disaster, but it was 14 April before her body was recovered by the Abertay Lightship. She was never to know her niece, the marathon runner Jenny Wood Allen.

The ill-starred Tay Bridge is also responsible for reminding us of William McGonagall's poetic ramblings. The opening of his memorial to the tragedy is as disturbingly familiar as the uncomfortable presence of its surviving pillars:

> 'Beautiful Railway Bridge of the Silv'ry Tay!
> Alas! I am very sorry to say
> That ninety lives have been taken away
> On the last Sabbath day of 1879.
> Which will be remembered for a very long time.'

Three years later, McGonagall trudged through snow to Balmoral to present a copy of his poems to Queen Victoria, but was left 'standing out in the cold' as a royal policeman told him, 'You are not poet to Her Majesty. Tennyson's the real poet to Her Majesty.' One can almost feel his hurt as he was turned back at the castle gates, a royal flea in his ear, pride dented and reputation savaged. Her Majesty thus avoided hearing the shimmering couplet he added later in his dramatic rhyme . . .

> 'And the cry rang out all round the town,
> "Good heavens! The Tay Bridge has blown down."'

There is a resurgence of interest in the world's best bad poet. Linda Caston showed that he was born in Ireland, not Edinburgh as previously recorded, his family reaching Dundee in their search for work. The Irish, when asked by the BBC and other media, felt disinclined to claim McGonagall as one of their own, and passed the poetic problem back to us. So the former handloom weaver, who 'discovered myself to be a poet in 1877', remains Dundee's best known figure on the world stage, an enigma deserving of historical revision. In recent times McGonagall has been resurrected by Spike Milligan,

Peter Sellers, the Monty Python team and the Muppets. His name at least seems destined to stay in public consciousness – something that would have tickled him pink.

Mary Slessor was another adopted Dundonian who found work in the town's mills, and another whose links to Dundee have undergone reappraisal. Slessor arrived from her native Aberdeen in 1859, aged eleven, undersize and barely able to write her name. Her journey from mill girl to missionary began on the death of David Livingstone in 1874, when a wave of missionary enthusiasm swept Scotland. In 1876, aged twenty-six, she sailed for Africa.

'Ma' Slessor, as she became known, spent the next forty years at the mission station of Calabar in Nigeria, facing incredible hardships and risking her life many times. She was greeted by poverty, slavery and exploitation and by fever and malnutrition. Rural areas were run by cannibal tribes whose existence was a nightmare of superstition and witchcraft. There she taught Christianity, child welfare and the principles of health and hygiene, and her influence extended over an area of 2000 square miles.

Slessor's death in West Africa in 1915 attracted worldwide comment, though curiously it drew only a short obituary in the *Advertiser*. Prolonging her memory is the Mary Slessor Foundation, which seeks to continue her work in Nigeria, and the presence of her portrait on a Bank of Scotland banknote. A commemorative stained-glass window celebrates her life in the McManus Galleries, which also has her personal bible and other belongings. A memory featured in my book *Daughters of Dundee* (1997) summed up the remarkable life she led. It told how she once went up-river into unexplored territory in a royal canoe, thirty-three huge native paddlemen in loincloths chanting songs in her praise to the beat of a great drum as jungle slipped past. And that was before she left Lochee!

8

1900 to 1950
CONFLICT AND CHANGE

The twentieth century began in Dundee like so many of the other nineteen – with the town in flames. A fire at Keiller's confectionery in 1900 caused damage of £70,000, wiped the Albert Square factory off the map and demolished the titbit hopes of a generation of sweet-toothed children. Panic-stricken girls escaped by the windows and 700 workers were made idle. Six years later, in the most destructive conflagration since the 1651 siege, a fire causing damage equivalent to £30 million today destroyed the six-storey Watson's bonded warehouse at the junction of Seagate and the aptly named Candle Lane. The blaze caused eerie purple, green and blue flames and ground-shaking explosions. Two million gallons of whisky went up in flames or down the drain. Rivers of it ran down nearby streets. As the inferno raged, the glow was visible from Brechin and Montrose and people on Dundee's outskirts could read newspapers out of doors at midnight.

These industries had no monopoly on major fires. The textiles trade was also vulnerable and the heavy smell of 500 burning bales at Eastern Wharf hung in the air as the century opened. And when Watson's Bond went up, down went two jute warehouses ignited by falling embers. Mill fires wreaked terrible damage and loss of life –

the worst in 1870 causing the death of four firemen at Gordon's flax warehouse in Trades Lane. Jute works had their own fire brigades as the bulky raw material was considered too precious to allow the town's fire service to damage it with water. But when big fires engulfed the city, prejudices were forgotten and it was all hands to the pumps. The century-old fire engine from the Camperdown Works Brigade – which helped its municipal brothers fight the Seagate Bond blaze in 1906 – is displayed in the foyer of brigade headquarters in Blackness Road.

Turn-of-the-century politics were a tad fiery, too. Three names come to mind – Alexander Wilkie, Winston Churchill and Edwin Scrymgeour. Wilkie is the least known of this fascinating trio. Since the passing of the Reform Act in 1832 Dundee had routinely elected Liberal MPs to its two parliamentary seats. In 1906 Alexander Wilkie broke the Liberal stranglehold by becoming one of the first two Labour MPs in Scotland. Punters gave Wilkie as much chance as Buffalo Bill, whose recent Wild West show on Magdalen Green had involved 600 men, roughly the level of support Wilkie was expected to secure. Against the odds, the trade unionist secured ten times that number to take one of the town's two parliamentary seats. The result, a watershed for his party, also revolutionised Dundee's political landscape. By and large Dundee has remained faithful to the Labour cause – red stickers spreading like measles across the town's estates at election time.

With Wilkie settled in, Winston Churchill arrived in Dundee in April 1908 to seek re-election to Parliament by standing for the city's other seat. By then, Churchill was a Boer War hero, a Liberal minister and a powerful political figure. As custom dictated, his elevation to a new post in Cabinet meant he had to put himself up for re-election. It was the policy then of the militant suffragettes to campaign in every by-election with the aim of ridding the country of the Liberal government, which had consistently refused their demands for votes. Emmeline Pankhurst herself promised Churchill a warm welcome to the city and he was awaited eagerly by growing ranks of women protesters, including twenty-seven national leaders, who took rooms in Lamb's Hotel in Reform Street.

Above all, the 1908 Dundee by-election is remembered for Mary Maloney's bell. Maloney was a London member of the Women's Freedom League who had taken part in various demonstrations. On one occasion she was carried on the shoulders of London dockworkers, and Churchill allegedly remarked that she had been drunk in the arms of the men. Maloney vowed to pursue Churchill to exact a public apology – which brought her to Dundee. Whenever Churchill spoke, Maloney produced a swinging dinner bell which drowned out what he was saying. The ding-dong exchanges were taken in fun initially, but some meetings had to be cancelled because of the uproar. Once Churchill avoided Maloney's bell by staging a meeting at breakfast time. Another time he made a speech in a shed to escape her.

Churchill duly won with a comfortable Liberal majority, while Mary Maloney's antics sparked a furious debate in the local press over whether the suffrage cause had been damaged through her independent action. In fact it served as a distraction from good work by local women and imported campaigners in a coalition of suffrage societies, which had attracted sympathetic crowds up to 10,000 strong. The entire Rangers team was even persuaded to wear 'Votes for Women' badges before a cup-tie with Dundee.

Churchill represented Dundee for fourteen years and much mythology has arisen from his association with the city. It has been said he swore that grass would grow on his grave before he would set foot in the city again. It has also been stated that the publisher D. C. Thomson (who called Churchill a loud-mouthed, characterless politician and accused him of trying to buy him off with an honour) swore that Churchill's name would never again be seen in print in his newspaper. Both oaths were a wee bit fanciful, although it is the case that Churchill never returned to Dundee. He certainly never forgot his rejection and the manner in which electors had turned against him. It was probably for this, as well as the infamous episode during the 1922 campaign when his wife Clementine was spat upon by local women for wearing pearls, that he turned down the town council's invitation in 1943 to offer him the freedom of the city. The dismissive note from a secretary read:

> 'Sir,
>
> I am desired by the Prime Minister to acknowledge your letter of October 8, inviting him to accept the freedom of the City of Dundee, and to thank you for your courtesy. Mr Churchill regrets he is unable to accept the honour which you have proposed to confer on him.'

Rubbing salt in the wound, Churchill accepted Perth's offer to confer its freedom on him four years later. Clearly he was determined to put behind him any personal association with the 'seat for life, cheap and easy beyond all experience' which had had the temerity to turf him out.

And Dundee has not forgotten his waygoing. A recent move to mark the centenary of his election victory in 1908 with a permanent memorial generated an 'overwhelming eighty per cent no' in a survey carried out by the *Evening Telegraph*.

If Alexander Wilkie broke a seventy-year Liberal stranglehold, and the suffragettes broke a few windows and once tried to strangle Winston Churchill, Edwin 'Neddy' Scrymgeour broke new ground in British politics as the nation's only single-issue Prohibition MP. Scrymgeour (1866–1947) was elected to Dundee Parish Council in 1898 as a Christian Socialist, preaching moderation and respectability. He fought for the poor and the weak, and later, as a Dundee town councillor, was instrumental in introducing a minimum wage for local authority workers – ninety years before Tony Blair thought of it. But throughout his political career Scrymgeour's passion and principal interest was alcohol prohibition – evident from numerous letters and personal documents in his as-yet-unsorted archives.

Prohibition involved the withdrawal of votes and influence from politicians and parties supporting the production and distribution of drink. Scrymgeour launched the National Prohibition Party in 1900. His Scottish Prohibition Party evolved independently in Dundee the following year, as a Christian party seeking to put forward parliamentary candidates who insisted on nothing less than the abolition of drink. Scrymgeour was its founder, secretary and organiser, and later became editor of *The Prohibitionist* newspaper, which commanded at the time a healthy circulation of 10,000 copies across Scotland. All members of his party had to be total abstainers, and its motto was 'Vote as You Pray'.

In the 'Churchill' by-election of 1908, Scrymgeour decided to stand for Parliament himself, possibly because no one else would take a public stand for alcohol abolition at a time when Dundee was no different from other working towns: the Friday delivery of wages coincided with drunkenness and rowdyism in its 389 public houses. It took a brave man to preach the evils of alcohol to Dundee's fighting-drunk, or to a shrieking sisterhood of mill girls barely able to stand. Despite a Cromwellian 'mandate from God', Scrymgeour came bottom of the poll. He stood unsuccessfully in the elections of January and December 1910 and failed again in 1918 – doubling the unpopularity of his ticket by espousing pacifism as well as prohibition during the First World War. It was in the General Election of 1922 that he finally prised Churchill from his 'seat for life' and was carried in triumph up Victoria Road to his tenement home.

The irony is that the Dundee newspapers kept the worst of their criticism not for Churchill but for Scrymgeour. It was the latter who was heckled, asked his views on putting a roof over Dundee or what size of teeth would be required to fit the mouth of the Tay. Ridicule followed him to Westminster, where he attempted to introduce a parliamentary bill to close down every pub 'instantly', and whereby all alcohol for medicinal purposes would only be sold in bottles labelled 'poison'. His bill failed. 'Neddy' Scrymgeour remains Britain's only Prohibition MP – either a top-drawer political prophet or a Dundee fruitcake, depending on your viewpoint. An attempt was made in 2002 to mark the eightieth anniversary of his election victory by calling on bars in the House of Commons to stop selling alcohol. That also failed.

Securing just half of Wilkie's 6000 Dundee votes in 1906 was a candidate normally far removed, literally, from the humdrum world of local politics. The young naval lieutenant Ernest Shackleton was better known across the country as a heroic polar explorer. Shackleton failed in his attempt to win a Dundee seat in Parliament, but he made friends in the city, whom he remembered with gratitude throughout his daredevil career. What he found in Dundee was a workforce that had built more polar exploration vessels than any other in the world, and when the golden age of exploration began in the early years of the twentieth century, Dundee shouted its pre-eminence from the mast-tops by constructing Britain's only purpose-built exploration vessel, the Royal Research Ship *Discovery*. Constructed in the Panmure yard of the Dundee Shipbuilding Company with traditional skills when wooden shipbuilding was becoming obsolete, and powered by engines from Gourlay Brothers, *Discovery* was the strongest wooden-hulled ship ever built. And when she was launched in Dundee in March 1901, the Antarctic expedition vessel carried the nation's hopes and the nation's hero, the lionised Robert Falcon Scott.

If the lucrative whaling trade of nineteenth-century Dundee 'owed its foundation' to such voyages of discovery, as one explorer wrote, the whaling industry certainly repaid the compliment to those seeking to satisfy their polar curiosity in the twentieth century. Dundee whaling ships were the choice of the A-list of explorers – not only Captain Scott, but also Shackleton, Nansen, Amundsen, Peary, Mawson and Byrd. The sturdy veterans of the Dundee fleet had sailed and steamed farthest north and farthest south by venturing from the known to the unknown as they plied their trade. It was therefore inevitable that they became the ships of conveyance for the world's explorers seeking the highest latitudes and public acclaim.

Dundee masters like Captains Thomas Robertson, William Guy, William Adams, Alexander Fairweather and Charles Yule were not only household names in Dundee – 'stout weather-beaten men who rolled along the pavements of the Nethergate and Reform Street followed by little boys' – they were famous names among anyone venturing beyond the 60th parallel north. They were said to know polar regions as well as the gateway of Earl Grey Dock. They were Arctic navigators and explorers in their own right with an impressive base of practical knowledge of the frozen regions. They had reached uncharted seas, discovered new lands, followed coastlines, observed weather systems, noted new wildlife and encountered unknown peoples as they added to the body of seafaring knowledge and contributed to the surveying of remote regions. But in the intense industry of each whaling operation, there was never time for headline-grabbing assaults on the roof of the world or thoughts of dramatic acts of personal achievement. As the teetotal Thomas 'Coffee Tam' Robertson put it, 'It is whales we are after, not geographical mysteries.'

The supreme prize of reaching the South Pole was never his, but Shackleton came to know Dundee and to regard it well. Invalided home from Scott's 1901 National Antarctic Expedition, he returned to the city in 1902, still only twenty-eight years old, to oversee the refit of the *Terra Nova* for the *Discovery* rescue operation, when 300 workmen gave up the 'Dundee Fortnight' holiday to refurbish the relief ship. In the General Election backlash against the Unionists in 1906, when the Liberals took fifty-eight of the seventy-two Scottish seats, Shackleton finished in a lowly fourth place. The defeat did not worry him unduly and two years later he set off again for his greater love, the Antarctic, which he christened, 'The birthplace of the clouds and the nesting place of the four winds'. And for his 1908 adventure, in which he planted the British flag 'Farthest South', he chose the Dundee-built *Nimrod*.

The *Terra Nova*, meanwhile, was not done with her Antarctic adventures. After relieving the *Discovery* in 1904 the Stephen's-built vessel was eventually sold to the Admiralty and became the headquarters ship for Captain Scott's epic journey to the South Pole in 1911–12. History has recorded how Scott's party all perished on their return from the Pole, but their ship soldiered on as the expedition conveyance and eventually returned safely. For her exploits in two major polar journeys in this heroic age, the *Terra Nova* of Dundee should be regarded among the elite of all expedition ships.

Shackleton's next ambitious plan, to cross the continent of Antarctica by foot, was hatched on return from the *Nimrod* expedition – for which he had become a national hero. When the expedition was announced early in 1914, Shackleton received nearly 5000 applications to join the adventure, from which fifty-six men were picked. Yet the proposed expedition was sadly short of funds. Shackleton wrote to the Dundee jute philanthropist Sir James Caird asking for a £50 donation. Caird promised him the staggering sum of £10,000 if he would come to Dundee to discuss the matter. The two men met in Caird's office, and after the project had been explained, the elderly, fatherly figure sent him an unconditional cheque for £24,000, equivalent to £1.7 million today, and almost the entire cost of the expedition. The explorer paid his last visit to Dundee in 1919 to make personal calls on some of the people who had supported him. Three years later he set out for the Antarctic for the fourth and last time. He never returned.

Local historians have borrowed a little latitude over the likelihood of Dundee's Preston Watson beating the Wright Brothers to powered flight in this turn-of-the-century period. I must consign this story to the receptacle already bulging with Dundee myths like the 'Dundee man drowns at sea' headline (under which, it is said, *The Courier* reported the *Titanic* disaster of 1912), Shakespeare's 'visit' to the town and the 'Marie-malade' explanation for marmalade's etymology. Those accounts which place Watson ahead of the pioneering Wrights, and the plaque at Dundee Airport which publicly advances the myth, are howlingly lacking in evidence. Powered flight was not an option for a provincial Scottish engineer in December 1903, when Orville and Wilbur Wright began our aviation adventure. It is a claim Watson never made himself and I doubt if the Dundonian achieved powered flight in 1904, 1905 or 1906 – though I will welcome evidence to the contrary. So let us not dwell on this assertion. Instead, it is worth acknowledging him as a skilled aviator who contributed to the development of powered flight, and who made the supreme sacrifice when he was killed near Eastbourne in 1915 in a Royal Flying Corps biplane, three months after obtaining his pilot's certificate.

Far more tangible to the people of Dundee was the 'rumbling sound' of the arrival of the motor car. The automobile had made its public debut in Dundee in 1897 – the first progress it made after turning the corner at

Albert Square was to run into the gutter. *The Courier* calmly reported, 'To start the car the driver had to work a winding-up arrangement at the side, and then connect the gearing with the wheels, when the car was supposed to go. The motor power is ostensibly petroleum, but, in reality, it yesterday consisted of a "physical" force of small boys who put their shoulders to the back of the car and made it move.' That two-horsepower engine of the 1890s sounds like my Citroën 2CV from the 1980s in which – *quelle horreur!* – I was booked for speeding on South Road. Somewhat slower was Alexander Watt, a Reform Street photographer who was allocated Dundee's first car registration number TS 1 in 1904 for his De Dion Bouton car, which he eventually made over to the city.

Great manufacturing centres rushed to meet demand and build their own cars – but the first and probably only Dundee-built car was the Werbell, constructed by the brothers William and Edward Bell. It had a twenty-five-horsepower engine and sold for the considerable sum of £520, equivalent to around £50,000 today, or the price of a BMW powered by 360 horsepower. Werbell production began from a factory in South Ward Road in October 1907, though it is thought only eight of the tourers were made. The following year, a Werbell made a 'first ascent' of the Law – about the time Preston Watson got into the air under his own steam. And by May 1908, girl racers had beaten hot-hatch boys onto the motoring map: a *Courier* car commandeered by cheering suffragettes outstripped another containing Winston Churchill.

That unruly race, the dash to the Poles, the rush to become airborne, and the racy political scene apart, the early years of the twentieth century in Dundee continued to revolve around its staple industry – the preparation, spinning, winding, weaving, calendering and finishing of raw jute. Turn-of-the-century Dundee remained a working-class, textiles-dominated city with a population that had risen to 180,000, Scotland's third highest after Glasgow and Edinburgh. Jute remained a powerful and influential industry, and strategically important – so much so that 'jute weaver' was a recognised trade occupation in the 1901 Census. It is really difficult to conceptualise this today, but in 1911 half of the working population of Dundee, some 41,000 people, were employed in textiles. It is an astonishing statistic. Imagine walking along the Murraygate and one in two passing people, including schoolkids, stinking of the stour of jute.

Mills and factories hummed, workers toiled, overseers intimidated with one glance and threw another syco-phantically at managers too busy clock-watching to return eye contact. Owners counted rising profits. How much they made is anybody's guess. Louise Miskell (2000) sug-gested that eleven of Dundee's thirty elite manufacturers left over £100,000 at the time of their deaths. This ex-tended to £200,000 left by Joseph Grimond and Robert Gilroy, to John Sharp and William Ogilvy Dalgleish, who each left over £700,000 (£44 million today), to millionaires such as David Baxter of Baxter Brothers, who curiously had remained faithful to linen production. No other city shared such a dramatic working characteristic of minor-ity rich, majority poor, or such intense localisation of an industry. And during the periodic downturns, when the contrast between the astonishingly wealthy jute manu-facturers and the idle demoralised hands was stark, no other town was like Dundee.

While it is true that the early years of the century witnessed some of the largest shipments of jute to the city, and as recently as 1990 the Manhattan Works of Sidlaw Yarns was the largest jute spinning mill in Europe, the massive expansion of the 1870s and 1880s belonged to the bygone golden age. The honour of being the leading world seat of jute production had been ceded to India. When Mahatma Gandhi began his non-violent civil disobedience campaign in 1919, there were eighty-nine jute mills in the Calcutta district alone, employing a third of a million workers.

With individual profits and power on the wane, seven senior Dundee companies amalgamated in 1920 to form Jute Industries Limited. By 1950, only thirty-nine jute mills remained of the 125 at the industry's peak. Just four new mills were built in Dundee in the twentieth century, including the Eagle Jute Mill in Dens Road, with its Art Deco façade. And by the 1900s, Dundee was no longer a one-industry town, inured and indifferent to all others. In late 1911, a bitter dockers' and carters' strike brought the deployment of 300 soldiers of the Black Watch, and the resulting fuel shortage led to 30,000 textile operatives being laid off. For the first time in a century, external factors had caused an interruption to production. Other trades quickly developed unionised organisation and power which no women-staffed jute mill could boast. The Dundee Operatives Plasterers' Society, for example, was a secretive closed shop of 100 members. It was said that no plasterer from outwith Dundee dared pick up a tool in the city. Its cloth-capped membership made up its own rules and regulations and orchestrated apprentice numbers to suit its own ends. It was said that as soon as plasterers wanted a holiday they got it by creating a 'fancied grievance' in the workplace. The plumbers' trade union was also powerful and, by the start of the First

World War, the engineering unions had five branches in the town.

No history of a community should ignore the impact of the Great War. It is distressing even now to record that the city lost 4000 men, an entire generation of its youth, in this dreadful conflict. When the battalions of the Black Watch marched from Dudhope Barracks, neither the men nor the cheering crowds who bade them farewell could have imagined the awful outcome awaiting a battalion Andrew Murray Scott described as 'sons, brothers, fathers, uncles, schoolfriends and neighbours fighting shoulder to shoulder'.

'Dundee's Ain', the 4th Battalion, suffered terrible casualties at the Battle of Loos, where twenty of the twenty-one officers were killed alongside 235 of the battalion's 423 men. Amid the slaughter, as his comrades in the 4th fell, Joseph Lee captured the cold horror of war in the dispassionate lines of *The Dead Man*:

> 'He lay unasking of our aid,
> His grim face questioning the sky,
> While we stood by with idle spade,
> And gazed on him with curious eye.'

Lee, a native of Dundee who edited the *People's Journal*, survived the horrors described in his written record and is today highly regarded among the eminent First World War poets, but the Dundee 'pals battalion' was fatally wounded. After Ypres the 4th was disbanded and amalgamated with the 5th Battalion. Not one household in Dundee was unaffected by the carnage at Loos. *The Dundee Advertiser* issued a *Dinna Forget* booklet to mark the men's sacrifice, which is also commemorated annually by the lighting of the Law beacon. A painful irony is that many of those lost in the trenches had jumped at the chance to join up. They were the kettle boilers. Enlistment had been their way to save face and regain self-worth.

There was further distress when surviving soldiers returned home to discover that the promised jobs did not materialise. In August 1920, ex-servicemen besieged Dundee Labour Exchange, angry over the cancellation of benefits. A charity kitchen served a noon 'jug and pitcher' queue of 1500 people with a pint of soup and one-tenth of a loaf. When it was announced during a coal strike that year that coke was to be rationed, police were called to control an angry mob at the Dock Street gas works. Around 6000 turned up with 'pails, tin baths, clothes baskets, ancient prams and a great fleet of soap box carts' to rummage for the precious fuel.

Despite obvious poverty, contemporary evidence suggests that money was circulating comparatively well in Dundee at the time. In February 1918 a British tank paraded through the town for the start of 'Tank Week'. Residents were told that the cost of a tank for the war effort was £5000 and were encouraged to purchase War Savings Certificates. At the end of the week, bonds to the astonishing value of £4.5 million had been taken up in Dundee, the second highest total of all British cities. The pledges equated to £25 per head of population, or around £600 today, compared with Edinburgh's £14 per head and Glasgow's £13 per head. Only West Hartlepool outstripped Dundee with donations averaging £35 per head of its 60,000 population. Then, when Victory Bonds were introduced early in 1919, the citizens of Dundee snapped up more than £1 million worth within a week. While it is usual and all too easy to say that the jute barons were committing some of their stashed cash, evidence suggests otherwise. Considerable savings potential existed among Dundee's working classes. In 1901, for example, there were 44,065 ordinary bank accounts in Dundee, equal to thirty per cent of the population. The UK average deposit was just over £4, while in Dundee it was in excess of £12, or nearly £900 today. And one third of all new depositors in Dundee were folk engaged in spinning, weaving, dyeing or engineering.

With the huge tank 'Julian' in position in Albert Square in February 1918, textile manufacturers in the city proudly pledged a total of £1700 for the war effort. After the final day of fund-raising the *Dundee Advertiser* noted that the city's jute owners had flexed their financial muscle: 'Jute fibres turned into strands of gold. There is no gainsaying the fact that the staple trade was to a large extent responsible for yesterday's magnificent rally.' The paper was correct in the sense that the staple trade had been generous. The £1700 donated by the jute barons was eclipsed by the £2000 donated by women members of the Mill and Factory Operatives' Union. I can imagine the girls in their spontaneous and largely unintelligible mill patois signalling to each other, while continuing to work at unremitting speed on noisy machinery, to keep their bank balances to themselves – lest managers were tempted to reduce wages. Sadly, the memories and actions of Edwardian mill hands are just as hard to discern. Little contemporary evidence of their experiences survive . . . the jokes, anecdotes, rhymes, chants, ballads, superstitions and traditions of the working classes can be glimpsed only fleetingly in surviving records.

It was during these difficult post-war years that

Dundee's roller-coaster political history took a determined swing to the left, and mob rule. In September 1921, *The Courier* breathlessly reported benefit-deprived crowds surging up and down streets, *The Red Flag* being lustily sung and an alarming Communist banner unfurled. Over three days of rioting, windows were smashed, the Lord Provost and his family were attacked, police made repeated baton charges, a number of shops were looted and mounted police clattered under the arches of the Town House to disperse rioters. In scenes resembling the Keystone Cops, taxis crammed with police flew up and down the town, trying to quell sporadic violence, but the disruption and destruction continued until the Parish Council agreed immediate payment of hardship funds. Even the two minutes' silent observance of the Armistice in November 1921 was disrupted by indignant ex-soldiers.

There was no surprise when Dundee provided the British Communist Party with its first Scottish organiser in 1923. Bob Stewart was a friend and former town council colleague of Neddy Scrymgeour and organiser of his Scottish Prohibition Party. He was also a conscientious objector. During the war he was court martialled four times and imprisoned four times. He emerged as a protest leader in 1923 when 30,000 textile workers in Dundee were locked out. In the biggest demonstration in the city's history, he led 50,000 people demanding money for food and clothes. He stood as a Communist in the parliamentary elections of 1924 and 1929 and attracted over 10,000 votes in his last electoral attempt in 1931. Stewart's memoirs, *Breaking the Fetters*, provide one of the best reminders of this extraordinary period of political upheaval.

Hardship fell upon the town again during the ten days of the 1926 General Strike, when only one tram ran in Dundee, no newspapers were printed and a record 20,000 volumes were borrowed from the public library in one week. The strike, which was regarded by the government as 'a challenge to the Parliament and the road to anarchy', led to a one-off joint edition of the *Advertiser* and *The Courier*, and then amalgamation, ending a century of independent production of the town's two morning newspapers.

At least there was a determined effort after the First World War to find a solution to Dundee's slum housing. The lingering legacy of Victorian jute expansion was the makeshift housing Lego-ed around it to accommodate its workforce. Overcrowding and poor sanitation were rife. One case presented to Dundee's housing department concerned 'Man and wife, four sons aged 21, 11, 9 and 1, two daughters aged 15 and 13, totalling eight persons in a single room'. Another showed a one-roomed house which was shared by a couple and five children, the house 'miserably furnished' and dirty, the husband idle, the wife a mill worker, who had given birth to ten children, four of whom had died, while one had been placed in an industrial school.

Investigators from the welfare group, the Dundee Social Union, were asked in 1904 to inspect over 6000 properties in the densely populated area between where Marks & Spencer is located today and the West Port. The inspectors discovered that the appalling housing conditions accounted for a huge range of diseases and 'probably' high levels of child mortality. The Union's investigators, led by the pioneering social worker Mary Lily Walker, concluded that this housing was the 'greatest domestic evil'.

Walker's 150-page report, published in 1905, and her subsequent study of housing in November 1912, were discussed in the House of Commons and incorporated in the 1917 Royal Commission on Housing. As one commentator put it, Walker's work 'reduced to figures the lives of the people. It told of employment and its vicissitudes, of wages and expenditure and of diet, of overcrowding, of the lack of sanitation, and the consequences thereof.'

In 1906, Walker launched the first respite restaurant for nursing mothers in Britain in an attempt to encourage breastfeeding. She also inaugurated the first School for Crippled Children, the Dundee Baby Clinic and the first Infant Hospital in Scotland. She is remembered today as the founder of the Grey Lodge Settlement, which provides help to the city in worthwhile ways in her former home. Essentially, she wrote Dundee's social services handbook. Her greatest legacy, the 1905 Dundee Social Union report, is requested more than any other document in Dundee's local studies library and the city council's archives department.

The first of the housing improvements became the most famous. The Logie estate, beneath Balgay Hill, began in 1919 as a response to the government's drive to build houses for returning soldiers and workers – the 'homes for heroes'. In Dundee, however, the new homes were viewed less romantically, as necessary to address its dreadful housing, described by the 1917 Royal Commission as '32,000 living in overcrowded conditions in Dundee'. Logie's four-flat blocks, planned by James Thomson and centred on a tree-lined avenue, offered a model that cleverly imitated upmarket villas and also departed from high-rise tenements and the fashionable 'garden village' workers' cottages created as a solution in England. Ahead of his time, Thomson had provided Scotland's first municipal housing estate and the first heated housing scheme in Britain. 'Where Dundee Leads' ran *The Courier*'s proud headline when Logie was opened in 1920.

Today, the spacious estate attracts eager town planners from far and wide, while there is renewed interest in the visionary city engineer and architect James Thomson. The pity is that workers had little opportunity to live in Logie. Such was its appeal that the houses were taken by the town's emerging middle classes – insurance workers, teachers, shopkeepers and bankers. A further irony is that Dundee Town Council, which led Britain in council estates through the development of Logie, never built a council house in the last quarter of the century.

Inspired, it seems, by Logie's success and Thomson's subsequent creation of Scotland's first garden suburb for the working classes at Craigie, planners embarked upon an ambitious scheme to create 'Greater Dundee'. The town had already, in 1913, annexed Broughty Ferry for its summer playground. In 1920, the city completed the purchase of 264 acres on Linlathen estate for £35,342. In 1925, the council bought the 228 acres of Dudhope estate for £18,000, overlooked by the Law memorial to the city's war losses, which was unveiled the same year. And in 1925 it purchased 117 acres of West Kirkton for £5250. The new lands of Greater Dundee were quickly earmarked for housing and industry. Two hundred council houses were completed at Taybank in 1924, and 280 at Craigie by 1928. The Fleming housing estate, opened in 1929, was the gift of the London merchant bankers Robert Fleming, whose founder was proudly a Dundonian, and grandfather of Ian Fleming, creator of James Bond. This provided a further 400 houses for working people in the Clepington area of the city. By the end of the 1920s Dundee boasted one of the highest proportions of house tenants in Britain. Today's city was taking shape.

What of the 1930s? What made the Scottish poet and writer Hugh MacDiarmid portray Dundee in 1934 as a 'grim industrial cul-de-sac' and 'a monument' to man's inhumanity to man? What influenced the eminent journalist James Cameron, who worked in Dundee in the 1930s, to record that it was a place of 'singular desolation' – or Lewis Grassic Gibbon to say in 1932 it could inspire Dante to improve his *Inferno*?

When Britain fell into the Great Depression in the early 1930s, urban manufacturing centres such as Dundee were badly hit. It is hard to imagine the grim hardship of 1931 and 1932 when the city's unemployed numbered 31,000 and 26,000 respectively (around 4000 unemployed in the city claim benefits today). Orders dried up, factories closed, thousands were made idle or thrown out of work. There was no system of benefits then and little help or hope for the long queues at the Labour Exchange. Even those lucky enough to retain work dreaded losing it, and often put up with poverty-level wages.

Once again, the situation proved fertile recruiting ground for the Communist Party. Among twenty-five arrested in Albert Square in 1931 was Mary Brooksbank, the political spitfire who evolved into gentle mill poet and one of the world's first protest singers. One of a family of ten living in a two-roomed house, Brooksbank recalled being kept from school to look after her younger siblings, even though her father was idle. By the age of eleven she was boosting family income as an underage shifter of bobbins in the Baltic Mill. Her first political role was providing tea to striking dockers in the 1911 strike. With unemployment over 30,000 in 1931 she took to the streets as a Communist Party recruit, incited a riot and was rewarded with three months in Perth Prison.

Brooksbank's secret writing only became public after she had retired to look after her invalid mother. She eventually published *Sidlaw Breezes* in 1966 when she was sixty-eight. *Nae Sae Lang Syne*, her autobiography, and a much rarer work, was completed when she was in her seventies and paid for out of her meagre resources. Brooksbank once described her poetry as 'political, pastoral and philosophical'. Her most famous lines, written while she was in Perth Prison, and now etched around the mill lassies' memorial clock in Murraygate, capture perfectly the three elements:

> 'Oh, dear me, the mill's gaein fast,
> The puir wee shifters canna get a rest,
> Shiftin' bobbins coorse and fine,
> They fairly mak' ye work for yer ten and nine.'

The crash of masonry heard in the city centre at the end of 1931 was not caused by Communist protest, but by the demolition of Dundee's 200-year-old William Adam Town House. This controversial act of 'civic vandalism' has been lamented by successive generations of the town's inhabitants, but was acceptable to its council then, not least because the four faces of its clock had the disconcerting habit of showing different times.

The Courier weighed up the council's dilemma: 'Is the Town House to remain as a monument to one of Scotland's greatest architects, a centre around which the

sentiments of Dundee citizens for generations have gathered; or is it to be wholly demolished, or transplanted
stone by stone so that an unobstructed view may be
afforded from High Street to the frontal of the new Caird
Hall?' The town librarian and prolific author A. H. Millar,
sometimes marginalised nowadays in terms of historical
accuracy, led the arguments for its retention, bravely telling his council bosses, 'The despicable Philistinism which
masquerades under the name of modern utility has lately
run riot in Dundee.' One wonders what Dr Millar, James
Thomson or, perish the thought, William Adam, would
have made of the Waterfront mess or the utilitarian but
universally despised Tayside House?

The prospect of much-needed jobs at the height of
unemployment in 1931 may have swayed the council to
push for its demolition. Or should the role of Sir James
Caird, the most wealthy and influential figure in the city,
be re-visited? The jute multi-millionaire's greatest legacy,
the Caird Hall, had opened in 1922, but was shielded
from wider view by the venerable Pillars. Possibly the
council was mindful of the sensitivities of the town's
leading benefactor when it reached a municipally expedi-
ent decision to condemn the building to complete
demolition against strong public opposition, paving the
way for today's City Square. And possibly this is why
Caird's sister Mrs Marryat, moved by the outcry at the
loss of the Pillars, provided last-minute money for the
hall's last-minute, colonnaded façade – one set of pillars
in compensation for another. So the first stones of the
historic building were removed on Hogmanay 1931. If
ever there was a case of burying bad news on a good
news day, this was it.

Historians and architects still lament the fall of the Town

Dundee '800' celebrations, 1991

Dundee High Street, 1994

Tay Road Bridge, 2006

Reform Street, 2006

Tayside House, 2006

Morgan Tower, Nethergate, 2006

D.C. Thomson building, Albert Square, 2006

Chamber of Commerce, Meadowside, 2006

Desperate Dan statue, High Street, 2006

Robert Burns statue, Albert Square, 2006

Murraygate, 2006

East Mill, Guthrie Street, 2006

House, but the clock cannot be turned back. In any case, one of its faces ended up set into concrete in a South Road garden. Panelling at Dens Park football stadium is said to have come from the Adam building; its chandelier was hung in the council chambers; and its stones were numbered and taken away . . . but where? Maybe they were stored in anticipation of James Thomson's idea to remove the Pillars stone by stone across the High Street where it 'could have been marvelled at from every compass point' – a proposal ultimately rejected by the town council. The majestic bridge proposed by the prescient Thomson, which would not have blighted the city centre as our present bridge does, was also rejected by blinkered councillors.

The 1930s had hardly moved forward when Dundee lost another of its historic meeting places, the Greenmarket. This wide area, between the rear of the new Caird Hall and the river, was the town's second-hand market, and where a Belgian reputedly sold Britain's first ever bag of chips. The Greenmarket was cleared away in 1936 to make way for Shore Terrace bus station, which itself was removed in the 1970s for Tayside House. Marketplace to bus station to monstrosity: questionable progress from the Waterfront-school of spaghetti architecture. Another casualty in this area was the Royal Arch, hurriedly erected in wood for Queen Victoria's visit in 1844, replaced by a stone copy, but finally levelled for the road bridge in the 'Great Knockin' Doon' of 1964. The following year, the adjacent West Station was pulled down in the misguided municipal push to ensure 'Dundee's bridge' made landfall in the city centre. As Charles McKean put it, 'Dundee preferred a bridge into Dundee and obliterated its central area and docks to make room for it.'

For obvious reasons, entertainment in the 1930s lay beyond the despondency of domestic confines. Across Scotland, hiking and biking clubs were formed to encourage outdoor activity for the masses. One enthusiast was Mary Brooksbank, who captured the wonderful sense of escape in the opening lines of *Cycling Days*:

> 'I will remember in the years left to me,
> Whirring wheels 'neath the fair blue sky,
> Sweet winds from the hills as we sped along,
> Together, you and I.'

Jenny Wood Allen, later a household name in the world of marathon running, initially took to two wheels. Jenny joined the Dundee Heather Belles women's cycling club in the 1930s and became a champion time triallist. She told me that 'sometimes' she would finish work early, 'and with a Mars bar in each pocket, and mainly on my own, I would cycle to Glasgow, meet some of the Glasgow girls, sleep in a barn, race on the Saturday morning, then cycle home.' Swimming clubs were also a popular route to escaping the drudgery of home life and work. The Dundee baths, on the riverfront, opened in 1910 and were known to the working classes as The Shorers. The three pools were heated to a chilly seventy-two degrees – hence the 'shivery bite' after-swim treats – but pampering could be had at the Foam Baths, Oxygen Baths, Turkish Baths or Aerotone Baths.

For the well-heeled, celebrity concerts at the Caird Hall featured opera greats Mario Lanza and Beniamino Gigli, singers Paul Robeson and Gracie Fields, entertainer Bob Hope and the diva Dame Nellie Melba, who claimed her mother was born in the city. For the workers, Dundee offered a refuge of 200 tables in public billiards halls by 1934, at one table to every 890 inhabitants the highest ratio in Britain. For the hard up, the Esplanade offered public promenading, which cost nothing, or a free climb to the long-overdue Mills Observatory on Balgay Hill, which opened in 1935, or entry to the 'museum of sorts' at Dudhope Castle. The gloom was lifted for rare holidays, such as the procession for the jubilee of King George V and Queen Mary in 1935, when 100,000 gathered in Baxter Park, and the 1937 Coronation celebrations, when the city's schoolkids received commemorative chocolate.

The most classless of activities, offering a hypnotic escape for the working masses, was a night at 'the pictures'. By 1930 Dundee's eight theatres had been converted to cinemas and 'talkies' had reached the town. The first to open was Peter Feathers' Stobswell Cinema Theatre in Morgan Street in 1910, which offered tea and biscuits with admission. One of the first films screened was a record of Dundee FC's Scottish Cup win that year. The sequel is awaited. This was trumped in 1911 by a blockbuster showing the rumbling production of *The Courier*, in which I am certain some of my present-day colleagues appear. By the 1930s Dundee had over thirty cinemas, the highest number per head of population in Scotland. There were chief projectionists, second projectionists, third projectionists, spool boys and apprentices, attempting to make the 2000-foot reels of film look continuous, though they needed changing every twenty minutes.

It was often 'standing room only'. To demonstrate the point, the manager of La Scala in the Murraygate was charged with allowing 305 standing in his cinema, 155 more than were allowed under his licence. An Eskimo was paraded on stage during *Nanook of the North* at the Kinnaird, and in 1925 a group of Tibetan llamas was led on at a screening of *An Epic of Everest* at the Palace. This coincided with a visit to the city of the Grand Lama of Gyantze, the third largest of Tibet's holiest old towns, who laid a wreath on the Law war memorial, at which point sunshine broke through heavy clouds. It was seen as a good omen for the troubled times.

And when Green's magnificent Art Deco Playhouse opened in 1936 with seating for 4100, its wide-eyed patrons were witnessing the biggest cinema in Britain. Writer W. Stiven recorded excitedly, 'There is a new one being built in the Nethergate which is capable of accommodating I forget how many thousands, or is it millions?' When Green's glass and steel tower was illuminated, it had the same effect as Cox's stack – it could be seen for miles, putting the gas of any rival at a peep. In these multi-screen days, redundant cinemas often provide a place of calling for bingo lovers. Green's, now Mecca, continues to be Kelly's Eye – and is probably the biggest bingo hall in the world.

Dramatic scenes from the Spanish Civil War, played out on Pathé newsreels at Green's, resonated with a hushed Dundee public. Between 1936 and 1938 around 100 men from the city joined the International Brigade in Spain. Sixteen Dundonians were killed in the fight against fascism. A memorial plaque in Albert Square records their sacrifice with the words that there is no finer cause in the world than 'the fight for the liberation of mankind'. Determined men were also marching closer to home in the 1930s. Dozens of Dundonians took part in long-distance protest walks over unemployment and food prices. On one hunger march to London, it took eighty men from the city a month to cover the 400-plus miles.

The pre-war gloom was lifted, literally, with Dundee's audacious attempt on the world long-distance aviation record in 1938. Largely forgotten today, *Mercury* and *Maia* were the upper and lower components of the *Mayo* composite 'pick-a-back' aircraft, designed in the 1930s as a long-range mail and passenger carrier. The larger seaplane's role was to help the lighter monoplane into the air to about 10,000 feet, when the device uniting the two was released and the *Mercury* rose clear of the mother craft and went on its way with enough fuel for a journey of 3500 miles, sufficient to take it to Cape Town in South Africa, a record distance.

The Tay estuary was chosen as the best take-off location in Britain for the record piggyback attempt. Delayed by the Munich crisis, when Chamberlain undertook cavalier negotiations with Hitler over the future of Czechoslovakia, the *Mercury* was mounted on the back of *Maia* by crane at King George V wharf, and in October 1938 the aircraft skimmed down the water and lumbered into the air, with thousands watching from the river's shores. It had been arranged that the separation point would be above the Law, but the huge crowds on the summit were disappointed. It took place somewhere between Auchterhouse and Forfar, before *Mercury* turned south on the record attempt.

Mercury failed to reach Cape Town in a single hop, being forced to land at the mouth of the Orange River, some 350 miles from its destination and 261 miles short of the non-stop record. It was, however, the longest flight by a seaplane – a record that stands. Its Australian pilot, Captain D. C. T. Bennett, fêted as a hero in Dundee, soon had other concerns, becoming Air Vice-Marshal Bennett and leader of Bomber Command's Pathfinder force. *Mercury* was broken up during the war. Its mother ship *Maia* suffered a direct hit from a German bomber while at anchor in Poole harbour.

As hostilities with Germany loomed, 4000 British Association scientists meeting in Dundee were hurriedly advised to return to their homes – their legacy a useful scientific study of the town. When war was declared on 3 September 1939, gas street lamps were extinguished and a complete black-out ordered – one Broughty Ferry resident was later jailed for ten days for showing house lights. Hospitals were evacuated to prepare for emergencies, cinemas and schools were closed as was any place where large crowds could gather. Football grounds closed – with Dundee top of the First Division. Dundee Rep, newly opened in Lochee, had to close. The Home Guard was mobilised and vulnerable children were prepared for evacuation to the safety of untargeted rural communities. By the summer of 1941, almost 20,000 local men had enlisted in the services, leaving fatherless homes which the city's chief constable lamented were causing the wild youth of Dundee to get 'wickeder and wickeder'.

Typical of the men who enlisted at Dundee Labour Exchange was Norman Blair, whose wartime memoirs were published privately in 2005. Blair swapped his job in a tailor's shop in Dundee for training to become an RAF air gunner, but was brought down to earth like many a 'rookie hopeful' by passing out as a ground gunner. First the twenty-year-old guarded airfields in Wales, enduring German attacks by day and night. Occasional leave in Dundee came and went and it was back to the war. Shipped to the Middle East, he saw active service in Egypt and Libya before walking 120 miles in a bid to avoid the German advance on Benghazi, until finally he was taken prisoner by Rommel's forces. Blair's twenty-first birthday was spent facing trigger-happy guards in a makeshift wire enclosure in the desert. He was shipped to Brindisi in southern Italy, and marched through spitting crowds to his first proper prison. Thereafter he was cattle-trucked to Fortress Gavi, the Italian equivalent of Colditz, where his skill on the accordion acted as a distraction for escape attempts, among them one by SAS founder Colonel David Stirling. Prisoner-of-war camps in Austria, Poland and Germany followed, where he made an audacious escape in 1945. Aged twenty-four, after 1172 days in captivity, he eventually made his way home, arriving in Dundee three weeks before VE Day.

Zoe Polanska Palmer's story also bears telling. Born and brought up in Russia, she was just thirteen when she was wrenched at gunpoint from her family and taken to Auschwitz, the largest Nazi death camp, where she was subjected to the experiments of the infamous Dr Josef Mengele. From 1943, when she was sent to Auschwitz, until 1945, when she escaped from Dachau, she suffered torture at the hands of the Nazis. She still had terrible marks on her hands when I interviewed her at her Broughty Ferry home in 2001. 'I was tied to a bed,' she recalled. 'They would come with needles. I was subjected to injections and transfusions, without knowing what they were for. It was petrifying.' When Polanska Palmer recorded her experiences in *Yalta Victim* in 1986, she was the first person in the West to publish an eyewitness account of what had happened in the Holocaust death camps.

These experiences were perhaps not typical of the Second World War, yet the hardship and sacrifice endured by Blair and Polanska Palmer in their very different captivities were far from unusual. Their stories, two of many, act as a reminder of what this Dundee generation – indigenous and incomer – endured for the greater good and on behalf of generations following.

The war also arrived on Dundee's dockside doorstep. Secret arrangements had been enacted for the submarine depot first established in 1908 to host most of the 2nd Submarine Flotilla, Britain's largest. It was from the depot that HMS *Oxley* sailed on patrol on 10 September 1939, just a week after war was declared. The *Oxley* became the first naval casualty of the conflict – but not the last to be lost to 'friendly fire'. Later in the war, the multi-national 9th Submarine Flotilla used Carolina Port as its home base, where it was inspected by General Charles de Gaulle in January 1943. The flotillas' comings and goings went unreported until 1945, by which time around twenty submarines were based on the Tay, used principally to prevent the German navy intercepting convoys to Russia. Was it coincidence that brought this Arctic maritime role to Dundee?

One submarine story that could not be kept submerged as a secret involved the German U-Boat U2323 which, in May 1945, glided up the Tay to surrender to an astonished policeman in the calm waters of Dundee docks. The crew had learned a day earlier of Germany's surrender.

Eclipsing that adventure is one of the most bizarre stories to emerge from the Second World War era. Jessie Jordan was married to a German waiter whom she had met at the Royal Hotel in Dundee. She learned the hairdresser's trade in Hamburg between the wars before returning to Scotland in 1937 to open her own shop, first in Perth, then in Kinloch Street, Dundee. Unknown to her customers and neighbours, Jordan had been recruited by the German Secret Service. Her main purpose in returning to Scotland was to take photographs and make drawings of Britain's coastal defences.

An assistant in Jordan's shop developed suspicions about her regular absences. She then came across a diagram of the Tay Bridge with the word 'Zeppelin' written on it – which may have been Jordan's code name. The police were informed and on a return trip to Germany in 1938, sailing from Dundee aboard the SS *Courland*, Jordan was tracked by officers from MI6. With Dundonians agog at the spying scandal unfolding in their town, Jordan, by then fifty-one, a blonde woman of medium height, was arrested on her return and charged with offences under the Official Secrets Act. At the High Court in Edinburgh she admitted photographing Southampton Docks and acting as a forward address for censored post. The most alarming aspect of her work was that she had made sketches of classified government installations and coastal defences, which could have led to bombardment in the years ahead.

Jordan was found guilty of spying and sentenced to four years' imprisonment. She was eventually sent to Holloway women's prison in London whose FPs (former prisoners) included Dundee suffragette Annot Robinson, jailed in 1909 for trying, Trojan-horse style, to enter the House of Commons hidden in the back of a furniture van. Jordan spent the entire war in captivity. She was repatriated to Germany in 1945 and died in Hanover in 1954. The irony of this John Le Carré-like drama is that Jordan's return to Scotland in 1937 was said by her to have been prompted by the people in Hamburg regarding her a British spy.

Dundee was earmarked as a target for the Luftwaffe and Kriegsmarine as early as November 1939, but there were few direct hits on the city during the war. Nearly 1900 local people lost their lives during the six years of conflict – many are now buried in some foreign corner. This was a source of great sadness, but there was no repeat of the mass losses in the trench warfare of 1914–18. Come VE Day in 1945, 50,000 residents found it possible to celebrate victory in City Square: local women were enticed to dance the day away by the charm of heel-clicking and bowing Polish servicemen.

In Dundee – now happily twinned with the German city of Würzburg, among others – the end of the war threw up a painful vision of what had happened in 1918, when men returned to no jobs and domestic penury. Because of this, and partly due to the severity of the war damage in the south of England, the government intro-duced dispersal-of-industry legislation. In the second half of the twentieth century this policy was to have a more dramatic physical effect on Dundee than anything since the siege of 1651.

9

1950 TO 2000
SHIPSHAPE!

The second half of the twentieth century began in similar fashion to the first. The traditional Dundee staples continued to paint familiar shadows across the employment canvas.

Jute remained Dundee's largest employer until 1966 . . . and survived as a manufacturing industry in the city until 1998 when the 'cinema'-fronted Tayspinners' Works in Morgan Street closed. Opened as Taybank Works in 1949, it was the last significant mill built for the once all-powerful textiles industry in the city. Most of Dundee's jute in the second half of the twentieth century became backing for tufted carpets, sacks and chair and wall coverings, but increasingly it was replaced by synthetic materials, such as rayon and polypropylene.

Keiller's, one of the best-known brand names in Scotland, did not escape the Second World War unscathed – its London factory was bombed during the Blitz. The firm continued the region's soft fruit and preserves industry from a factory at Mains Loan, which opened in 1947. There production was concentrated on marmalade for export to dozens of countries in small jars and ceramic pots; jars which once rained down from upper windows during Communist riots today excite collectors and eBay buyers. The firm had already lost its local independence when it was taken over by Crosse & Blackwell. In 1961, the famous family name passed to the Nestlé group, and the last factory in the city closed in 1988, when marmalade production was transferred to Manchester.

D. C. Thomson had been forced by wartime newsprint supply shortages to curtail production, to publish some titles fortnightly instead of weekly, and to reduce the size of several publications. Many staff members enlisted for active service. And yet the seeds had been sown in the 1930s for the boom in children's papers, which awaited their return to journalistic duty. The company emerged from the war on the cusp of one of its most successful periods. Its backbone of newspapers, which included the *Sunday Post*, *Courier & Advertiser*, *Evening Telegraph*, *People's Journal* and *Weekly News*, was flourishing. Comics such as *The Beano* and *The Dandy* were on their way to becoming national institutions; boys' papers like *Hotspur*, *Wizard*, *Rover* and *Victor* had legions of baby-boom boy fans, while teenage girls across the country found their lives shaped by *Romeo*, *Jackie* and *Blue Jeans*, all produced on the editorial floors in Meadowside. *Jackie*, which rolled off the presses in 1963 and peaked at sales of over one million, with a potent mix of boys, bands, fashion and features, continues to engender special affection – though not with this author, who lost the girl in a *Cathy & Claire* problem page photo shoot in April 1974.

Between the Seagate and the river, modern Dock Street, were the yards and foundries of Dundee's diminishing shipbuilding industry. Stephen's, Gourlay's and Dundee Shipbuilders had passed into history, but the Caledon battled on at the Stannergate before closing acrimoniously in 1982 after 107 years of building ships. One of its last jobs was to construct the box girders for the Tay Road Bridge. Gourlay's 1870 cast iron-framed, A-listed engineering foundry in East Dock Street, where the engines for *Discovery* were built, and where Preston Watson is said to have constructed one of his prototype flying machines, was recently rebuilt on an adjacent site for retail use.

Instead, new industries were to revolutionise where Dundonians worked and lived. According to the satirical weekly *Piper of Dundee*, the writing was on the wall for jute as early as 1892. It commented that year, 'There are a hundred and one industries which would yield better returns than the speculative jute trade, but Dundee still looks askance on such ventures.' It added that Dundee had 'acquired a Micawber-like attitude of waiting for something to turn up'. And that's when the city still employed 40,000 jute hands. By 1971, only 6000 remained in a drastically contracted industry run by fewer than twenty companies. By 1991 only four mills remained. And yet the Dundee of the 1950s and 1960s enjoyed unprecedented full employment at times. Post-war Dundee did not experience the lack of opportunities of 1918, but the dawn of a you've-never-had-it-so-good manufacturing revolution.

When the Luftwaffe flattened great swathes of London and other industrial cities in the early 1940s, there was a move to protect British industry by relocating firms from bombed-out sites to provincial centres. The government also attracted an influx of major overseas manufacturers to stiffen the economic regeneration. Through the 1945 Decentralisation of Labour Act, Dundee was awarded Development Area Status. That year, the Board of Trade enlarged upon this in a letter to Lord Provost Sir Garnet

Wilson: 'The great dependence of Dundee on the jute industries constitutes a problem which the Board of Trade fully recognises . . . and it is clear that a more balanced distribution of industry would be welcome.' To this end the Board of Trade was empowered to build factories and to lease them to approved tenants. Within a quarter of a century, from the point in September 1942 when 'only 442 people were working in the new concerns', inward-locating companies broke Dundee's traditional textiles stranglehold to account for nearly 12,000 new jobs.

Burndept and Hamilton Carthartt were typical new-comers. Burndept Ltd made batteries for wireless equipment used in tanks and aeroplanes. When its Kent factory was bombed in April 1941, lorry-loads of twisted metal and six essential workers arrived in Dundee and were deposited on a former jute factory site. Soon Burndept's Dundee factory was the largest dry battery plant in Europe, and when it became Vidor Ltd in 1961 it employed over 1000 people – with, as personnel officer, former prisoner of war Norman Blair. It closed in 1983.

The Canadian textiles company Hamilton Carhartt Ltd moved from Liverpool to Dundee in 1942 as part of the dispersal legislation. By 1951, it was making one million garments a year, principally denim overalls for industrial purposes. In 1970, the company began producing Wild-cat jeans, and its workforce rose to 700. Although declining orders saw its Dundee operations close in the 1980s, the American jeans company Levi Strauss contin-ued the tradition by employing 500 workers at Dunsinane Avenue, and this award-winning factory survived to 2002.

In the 1950s, denims were as *de rigueur* for Dundee teenagers as they were elsewhere. It was in the Dundee pharmacy firm of Johnston and Adams that the recipe for Slipperine was concocted, and post-war teenagers by the thousand used the slippery stuff to dance the night away in Dundee's twenty-four licensed dance halls. In the JM Ballroom in North Tay Street, 10,000 people watched Pitlochry man Bobby Cannon dance the twist for ninety-one hours, earning prize money of £101. Hopefuls stayed off work for the competition. Some lost their jobs. And denim was fashionably flaunted when gangs of youths broke down the doors of the sold-out screening of *Rock Around the Clock* at the Empire Cinema in 1956.

Continuing the American theme but updating rockers to petrol-heads, Veeder Root of Connecticut arrived in Dundee in 1947 after a site battle with Wales. By the 1950s the US company occupied a large factory on Dundee's new Kingsway industrial estate and by 1968 it had extended seven times, primarily to manufacture counting and computing devices for use in garage forecourt petrol pump heads. In 1980 it had a workforce of 1200, which reduced in stages until it closed in the early 1990s.

Into this 'cool' era came the Astral Company, which set up in Marine Parade in 1945 and grew to become Britain's leading fridge manufacturer. Astral became part of the Morphy Richards group in 1955 and made spectacular headway. By 1961 it had four factories in Dundee with a workforce of 1600. Its eight-acre factory at Gourdie was the largest single factory in Scotland. It churned out its 100,000th fridge in 1963, while spin-dryers rolled off the production line at its Longtown Road factory at a rate of one every two minutes. Close by, US-owned Holo-Krome constructed an extensive factory in 1954 and then built its name and reputation on the manufacture of an extraordinary range of socket screws, while the 650-strong workforce of Ferranti Ltd contributed to the development of Concorde. On the eastern side of the city, French tyre giant Michelin established another significant presence, adding to the international dimension of the city's business base.

The most controversial of the incomers, eventually, was the American giant Timex, which began its links with a factory for wristwatch assembly at Dryburgh in December 1946, introducing what it called 'a brain machine' in 1961, probably the first computer in the city. At its peak in the 1970s, the Timex workforce of 6000 was producing innovative items such as digital watches, the revolutionary Polaroid Instant and Nimslow 3-D cameras, and Sinclair computers. By the 1980s, the company was still the city's biggest single employer. However, Timex also developed a reputation for poor industrial relations and at one point in 1983 workers barricaded themselves inside the company's Milton of Craigie factory for six weeks. After a bitter lock-out in 1993, Timex closed its remaining factory in Harrison Road and withdrew operations from Dundee.

One company which rolled with the blows and survived is the National Cash Register Company, otherwise NCR, which arrived from Ohio in 1946 to produce accounting machines and cash registers. It, too, was eventually faced by dinosaurian extinction amid declining order books, industrial unrest and a workforce that had tumbled from a peak of 6500 to just 1000 by 1977. But 'The Cash' refocused on research, and developed self-service technology so astutely that it won almost every prize available for exporting, while also being named Best Factory in Britain.

The sublime metamorphosis of NCR from a labour-intensive producer of mechanical shop tills to a world-wide leader in hole-in-the-wall cash machines, or ATMs, typified the winds of change blowing through Dundee's industrial landscape. By the mid-1990s, NCR employed 1500 in Dundee and had a third of the international market for ATMs, including a virtual monopoly of cash machines in Scotland. As the Lord Provost at that time, Mervyn Rolfe, put it, 'Summon money from a cash dispenser in Red Square or Times Square, chances are you're interacting with a little piece of Dundee.'

Industry can perform somersaults, too. When the Dundee family food giant William Low was swallowed up by Tesco in the summer of 1994, *The Courier* described it as the 'Death of a Dundee Dynasty'. The *Evening Telegraph* predicted doom and gloom, job losses and the end of an era. A decade on, Tesco was employing more people in Dundee than William Low ever did, and yet at the time of writing the company's desire to remove its distribution activity to Livingston suggests another important industrial site on the Kingsway artery will soon be vacant.

These big-hitting newcomers changed the face of manufacturing in Dundee. They transformed the post-war city from a mono-industry town into a modern manufacturing centre spread over several purpose-built sites along its northern ring-road. New horizons were presented, and it can be argued that the city adapted rapidly and did surprisingly well to hold on to these household-name companies for so long. Michelin and NCR remain stable employers of large numbers, the former recently cementing its roots in the city with construction of the largest urban wind turbines in the world. Timex, NCR, Holo-Krome, Vidor and Veeder-Root all enjoyed more than forty years of production in the city. I could argue forcefully that this was principally due to their cleverness in asking Dundee's largely female jute workforce to lay down its textile apron and don factory overalls, to move from city centre mills to industrial estates, and from spinning frames to circuit boards.

The dexterity of Dundee's daughters in this unrecorded period of Dundee's industrial history helped to transform the city's industrial backbone. Yet the same Dundee women staged a long and angry protest outside Timex's Harrison Road factory gates in 1993, at a time when strikes in the UK were at their lowest level since 1926. The dispute clattered across television screens and newspapers, the banners, huts and 'intifada' caravan on Harrison Road portrayed as the last roar from a dinosaur long defeated. The altercation was compared to the acrimonious scenes over union recognition at Grunwick in 1977, the national miners' strike in 1984 and the infamous Wapping newspaper dispute in 1986. There were violent incidents, dozens of arrests and the media imposition of a depressing new reputation as a city held in an industrial time-warp.

Dundee's image, never very favourable, was dented once again. Women formed over 300 of the 340-strong workforce who were sacked and later locked out by management, but men dominated the dispute, notably male officials of the Amalgamated Engineering Union. Not for the first time, the city's working women were largely divorced from decision-making. There exists the possibility that had women been given better access to negotiations, the American company might not have closed its Dundee factory and withdrawn from the city in 1993.

Dundee's post-war industrial revolution increased the number of people abandoning the jam-packed city to live closer to peripheral factory sites – at one point squatters occupied the 100-roomed jute baron's mansion of Castleroy in Broughty Ferry in a protest over inner-city overcrowding. Between 1945 and 1947, the city constructed 1550 prefabricated houses as a temporary solution to the urgent shortage. Most of the original allocation went to families whose men were coming out of the forces – the first prefab in Strips of Craigie in 1945 went to a war-wounded veteran taken prisoner at St Valery in 1940. His new rent was 10s 5d a week (52p), with rates of 3s 7d a week (18p), making 14s a week (70p).

The 'instant' two-bedroom homes, with little gardens and corrugated sheds, inspired affection among former tenement dwellers. Among husbands there was a great swapping of mowers, graips, and garden know-how. Wives borrowed sugar and nattered over hedging. Bairns exchanged sweetie coupons and used 'No Football' noticeboards as goalposts. On the downside, prefabs shared a common problem with dampness. Roofs leaked, windows trapped condensation and metal frames corroded. Adding to the pariah status of prefabs was the asbestos sheeting used in their construction. Gradually, whole schemes were earmarked for demolition. In 1970, Dundee Town Council decided the remaining ninety in their housing stock should go – twenty-five years after the predicted end of their lifespan.

With the pattern established, those who could afford it moved in droves from the decaying heart of the city to the brave new world of indoor lavatories on the city's boundaries. 'Model' estates – like the 3000 homes at Fintry between 1949 and 1960, and the 1200 homes at Charleston, finished in 1960 – were planned and quickly constructed. Over 1000 houses were built at Kirkton, and over 4000 at Douglas and Camperdown. Later Menzieshill, Ardler, and Whitfield, with another 5000 homes, made more room for a population hitherto confined to unwanted city tenements. Many had to cross James Thomson's Kingsway, Britain's first inner ring-road, to reach the new estates and the schools and corner shops that followed.

Another high-profile development took place closer to the heart of the city. In 1959 Dundee University's tower building in Perth Road butted into Dundee's chimney-dominated skyline. The ten-floor tower shouted the gospel of modern architecture – and the council was listening. High-rise flats seemed to be the answer to the city's housing crisis. In January 1960 the ten-storey Dryburgh block became the first municipal multi, followed by the Hilltown, Menzieshill and Ardler schemes. By the summer of 1980, fifty-five multi-storey blocks towered over the city, providing 5087 homes for a population equivalent to a town the size of Forfar. By then, though, planners and public had agreed that decanting householders from inner-city tenements into brutalist blocks did not necessarily solve housing inadequacies. The policy was further contradicted by experience as social malaise turned many of the new schemes into near-ghettos. Physical appearance deteriorated, back gardens resembled refuse dumps, front areas were overgrown with weeds and dirty stairways daubed with graffiti. Tenants complained about the lack of shops and social facilities.

People's aspirations also changed. In the dawning age of consumerism and personal ownership – televisions, fridges, washing machines, cars – more wanted the good life among the rasps and the neeps, not life in an estate isolated from services and blighted by teenage gangs. And they wanted out of schemes like Fintry where it was common to have dozens of houses lying empty, Mid Craigie, which was known as Little Moscow, and Menzieshill, once dubbed Manhattan because of its towering skyline, but renamed Mushroomhill because so many tenants had damp houses. Life had moved on – the desire to be detached had arrived.

As I write in 2006, the number of multi-storey blocks across Dundee has almost halved. Huge crowds have gathered with cameras poised as block after block has been blown back to dust. Since the early 1990s, the demolisher's hammer has also swung on surplus council stock at Beechwood, Kirkton, Ardler and recently Charleston. One-time showpiece estates such as Trottick and Mid-Craigie have witnessed swathes of demolition, and private developers have been encouraged to move in and construct low-density homes. Perhaps the highest-profile unwanted properties to go were the deck-access blocks of the Skarne in Whitfield – whose reputation once advised all who entered to abandon hope. This was a watershed in reforming the image of the city's troubled estates.

One dynamic which arose from this civic cleansing was the pressure on Dundee's boundaries. Where did 450 families move to when Beechwood bit the dust? What of the 15,000 who lived in Whitfield before the bulldozers moved in? What became of the average 200 families in each demolished tower block? The irony is that Dundee's perfectly laudable drive to improve its housing stock contributed to its own population decline.

The clock could not be turned back. Unscrupulous

landlords could not shoehorn as many tenants as possible into the now-commercialised city centre. Neither could city planners go upwards, squeezing families into small building sites or unpopular skyscrapers. And where once there had been a long waiting list for local authority housing, late-twentieth-century Dundonians wanted their own homes with garages and gardens, with space for decking, barbecues and trampolines. Moreover, private developers had little access to brownfield sites within the squeezed city to build the low-density, tree-screened, high-quality homes demanded by today's first-time buyers and house movers. By the millennium, the stock administered by the council and housing associations had tumbled to 20,000 houses, half of what it had been a quarter of a century before. The dual effect on the city has been the swallowing up of former greenfield sites – such as the former Liff and Strathmartine hospital grounds – and local authority pressure on the Scottish Executive to widen its boundaries. As the millennium approached, this served at times to strain relations with neighbouring Angus and Perth and Kinross councils over the possible poaching of high-revenue, middle-class borderline communities such as Monifieth and Invergowrie.

What of the post-war city centre? Manufacturing had moved out, to be replaced by retailing, smaller businesses and service industries, best represented architecturally by the 1950s Guardian Royal Exchange building in Albert Square, with the brickbat for blandness going to the dismal Willison Street telephone exchange of 1958. Come the 1960s, Dundee was to witness a change that had the same effect on its inhabitants as the loss of William Adam's historic Town House twenty years earlier.

In the way that Tayside House is top of the blow-it-to-smithereens wishlist, the old Overgate is Dundonians' favourite candidate for restoration. It was demolished in the 1960s to make way for concrete Overgate 2, which preceded the present glass-fronted Overgate 3, opened in 2000. The old Overgate was supposedly the pounding heart of the town. The *Courier* columnist Jim Crumley once described it as 'The quintessential artery of Dundee, a vessel for the conveyance of civic lifeblood from the urban heart to every vital fibre of us all.'

In a polemically-cheeky *Courier* article a week later I called Jim's comments 'retrospective nonsense' and questioned why a 'virtual' version of the higgledy-piggledy Overgate had outlived its physical presence to attract such an outpouring of nostalgia. Dragging imaginary wagons in a circle around me, I suggested that evidence showed that the Overgate was a congested slum whose appalling accommodation was about as desirable as the plague which had slaughtered the medieval people buried ten feet below it. Conjure up as many romantic pictures as you like, nostalgically revisit it as often as you want, but the records show the Overgate was a crumbling, decaying, unhealthy blot on the local landscape. And when it came to crunch time, Dundee Town Council grasped the earliest possible opportunity to flatten it, which they did fifty years ago. Strange that there was hardly a dissenting voice when it was pulled down. Sure, today's wishful thinkers see the old Overgate as a cobbled street from a Hovis commercial, with a cute conglomeration of buildings, closes, garrets, with steps up to some, steps down to others. They do so through rose-tinted spectacles. It was the consumption capital of the city, a den of criminality and drunkenness and bairns sleeping in sinks because of filthy overcrowding. So there.

A less controversial but no less emotional city-centre change has been the passing of traditional department stores. At one time three locally-famous family retailers dominated corner sites at the Murraygate/High Street/ Commercial Street junction – Smith Brothers, G. L. Wilson and D. M. Brown, later Arnotts. When G. L. Wilson closed thirty-five years ago it was almost like a death in the family. Everybody shopped at The Corner, as it was known. The Edwardian D. M. Brown opposite boasted an 'indoor street' arcade and a pillared tearoom featuring carved Italian marble and the largest sheet of curved glass ever manufactured. Smith Brothers, famous for once supplying complimentary bowler hats to the town's sixty cabbies, provided seventy-five years of service before closing in 1970. A replacement in the Murraygate was Marks & Spencer, whose white 1960s façade was designed by Robert Lutyens, son of Sir Edwin Lutyens. In the High Street, Draffens, on the corner of Nethergate and Whitehall Street, was Draffen and Jarvie in 1899, before becoming Draffens of Dundee in 1948. It was a stylish meeting place where the manager would dust down the banister with his white handkerchief prior to opening. In 1981, when it was taken over by Debenhams – now trading from the rebuilt Overgate – local shoppers mourned the passing of a family firm which numbered the late Queen Mother among its customers. More recent departmental departures from the city centre include C&A and Littlewoods, while once-familiar retailers have also melted away. A 1965 snapshot of Murraygate would include, for example, Smith Brothers (outfitters), Scott (furriers), Etam (ladies' wear), Andrew G. Kidd (bakers), Rentaset Ltd (TV hire), McGregor (grocers), Grafton (children's wear), Jackson (tailors), Hepworth (clothiers), Bracken (fabrics), Dunn (hatters), Stevenson (dyers) and Potter (shoemakers).

Walk along today's busy Murraygate and if your eyes aren't drawn to shop fronts, people walking dreamily, dozily or druggily towards you, or the buses which crazily criss-cross the pedestrian zone, a bit of the city's past will stretch before you. The lingering tramlines fondly recall the last of the landlocked galleons careering along the city's streets. In the evolution of Dundee's urban transport, horse-drawn carriages gave way to steam-propelled cars in 1877, which were superseded by electric trams in 1900, which in turn met a fierce rival in buses, introduced in 1921. According to a sixpenny booklet published in 1936, the town's trams were 'lovely electrically-driven and electrically lit cars de luxe which we can now enjoy with so ample accommodation both inside and on the saloon on top, where one can smoke in comfort – having first, of course, asked permission from any ladies who have ventured to climb the "smoking room"'. At their peak in the 1930s, seventy-nine tramways were in operation around the city.

But mid-twentieth-century Dundonians considered trams old-fashioned, costly to run, too slow and an impediment to the growing volume of other traffic – just as the city's ancient gates had presented a traffic obstacle to increasingly-pompous carriages two centuries earlier. One survey in the early 1950s showed that ninety-five per cent of daily passengers in Dundee preferred buses to trams. So in 1956 what remained of Dundee's one-time fleet of double-deck trams was sold off as scrap – the last tram coming to a halt at one minute past midnight on 21 October of that year. Inquiries over whether they could be reintroduced to Dundee's streets have come to nought, but with civic fathers and mothers looking at ways to ease the commuter traffic burden on the city and its impact on the environment, priorities for better public transport usually involve a hazy timetable for the re-introduction of these clattering urban giants.

Other twentieth-century casualties included the Tay ferryboats, which sailed for the last time in August 1966, ending what was probably around 250 years of regular paid-for crossings between Dundee and Fife. Two of the last 'Fifies', the *Scotscraig* and the *Abercraig*, were removed to Malta in 1968 and could still be seen, though in considerable distress, until recent times. A more forgotten aspect of harbour trade is the roll-on/roll-off freight ferry service to Rotterdam, which used Dundee's eastern wharf from 1985. This was Scotland's first direct international ro-ro service, but the loss-making ferry lasted only six months – and went out in some style with an embarrassing grounding in a gale in the mouth of the Tay. And when Dundee cast a net in the following decade for a direct passenger ferry to Europe, it was cut adrift as Rosyth became the preferred east-coast port for Continental travel.

There were arrivals as well as departures. The new Tay Road Bridge saw 15,000 cars pass over it on its opening day in 1966. Grandads and grandmas who had never left their hearths for years were driven across to see the view from the other side. When the bridge was planned, it was envisaged that 10,000 cars would cross it daily. Around 24,000 now pass over it every day, with around £3.5 million in tolls collected annually. The assurance that tolls would be scrapped when capital costs were paid off had as much substance as recent promises of civil service jobs. Today, in 2006, *The Courier*'s campaign to end bridge tolls is winning public and political support across the country. In cleared space around the bridge landfall went the Olympia leisure centre (1974) and Tayside House (1976), while major buildings from this era in the now-divorced city centre included the grim Angus Hotel (1964) and the much-refurbished Overgate (1963) and Wellgate (1977) shopping centres.

A timely incomer was RRS *Discovery*, who returned to her home port in 1986, with thousands lining the Tay to watch her arrive piggyback on a floating dock. Later purchased outright for a nominal £1 by Dundee Heritage Trust, *Discovery* forms the centrepiece of an acclaimed museum in the berth which used to house the Fifies. Captain Scott once boasted it would take a nail the size of a javelin to pierce her bows, but he did not anticipate the funding leaks which the royal research ship would encounter on her return. Counterbalancing and outweighing this, *Discovery* has acted as an icon for the transformation of the city's image in the post-jute era. In 1996 Dundee was rebranded as the City of Discovery, and the ship continues to be an inspiration for those viewing for the first time her famous bows pointing northwardly.

If *Discovery* is the showpiece legacy of Dundee's maritime industry and synonymous with the city's outward-looking ambition, the timber-roofed frigate *Unicorn*, half a mile downstream in Victoria Dock, is the city's Cinderella ship. One of a handful of the world's oldest wooden-hulled warships, *Unicorn* has steered herself safely through the centuries since 1824, when she was launched, bristling with cannon. Overtaken and outclassed by steam power, she never saw action. She was initially laid up in Britain's reserve fleet, became a powder hulk at Woolwich Arsenal in 1857, then in 1871 was offered as either a training ship for destitute boys in Belfast or a cholera ship to be berthed off Rochester. Her ignominious career ended when she was towed to Dundee to become a naval reserve drill ship. She lies off the beaten tourist tack, while a succession of gentlemanly old salts come up with plans to prolong her remarkable survival, knowing in their own bones that if she had seen action, she probably would not be with us.

From the safe anchorage of the author's desk it seems clear that it would have been sensible for Dundee to concentrate its maritime memorabilia on a single site. *Discovery* is berthed at Discovery Point; the ninety per cent original *Unicorn* in Victoria Dock alongside the unfinished North Carr lightship from 1933; one of the world's earliest maritime instruments, an astrolabe dated 1555, in the McManus Galleries; a magnificent, Category A-listed Customs House in Dock Street; a whaling exhibition at Broughty Castle on the eastern edge of the city; Admiral Duncan memorabilia five miles away at Camperdown House on the west; and a large skeleton of the 'Tay Whale' somewhere in storage. Together they would comprise and be considered a world-significant heritage group of UNESCO standard and offer Dundee a stunning visitor attraction. Pie in the sea, perhaps. What would be nice to do is not always what is practical. There are always ownership and funding issues, and so they remain scattered. What did happen at the dockside, though, was the sell-off by Forth Ports of prime waterside land for housing, and some rather uninspired flats. Frustrating, isn't it?

While the broad estuary has provided the conduit for the town's commercial activity over the centuries, the river today is underused and arguably undervalued. Leisure activities are restricted to small-scale yachting, windsurfing and very annoying jet-skiing. The estuary's potential, however, was seen when the Tay hosted a round of the World Offshore Power Boat championship in the summer of 1994, and when it welcomed three participants in the Tall Ships Race three years later. A water festival made economic waves for a while; otherwise, the mindset for marine events does not appear as wide as the Abertay sandbar. It is not that the powerful presence of the river is ever forgotten, however. Putting to sea has always been a risky business. This was thrown into sharp focus in December 1959 with the loss of the *Mona* lifeboat crew who had launched from Broughty Ferry after the North Carr lightship broke her anchors in high winds. All eight lifeboatmen perished, a tragedy the city mourned for many months.

One of the most significant and welcome late-twentieth-century changes to Dundee took place away from the river. In 1966 the Perth Road campus of St Andrews University became the University of Dundee. It would be fair to say that the new university struggled at first to find its feet – not least when its student newspaper *Annasach* revealed in 1970 that 300 students had experimented with cannabis and LSD. But a fully formed world-beater emerged from this one-time chrysalis of Scottish higher education. Its current principal and vice-chancellor, Sir Alan Langlands, has overseen unprecedented levels of research grants, routine five-star assessments, record numbers of students, and three of his knighted life sciences boys in the UK's top fifteen cited scientists. Langlands has also engineered the virtual demolition and rebuilding of the Hawkhill area for campus expansion. But he is plainly not daft. He reminded me once, 'New buildings aren't the answer to everything. Fleming discovered penicillin without having a new building.'

The first cohorts of new graduates from Dundee University included former NATO Secretary General Lord (George) Robertson, who told me in an interview, 'I don't think I could have conceivably imagined when I was a student here and in my wee flat off the Perth Road that I would end up heading one of the world's most important organisations.' The political commander of the world's biggest arsenal of nuclear weapons conveniently omitted that he also led a student sit-in at the university's library.

Meanwhile, Abertay University has commandeered much of the old city centre around Bell Street for its expansion to accommodate upwards of 6000 students. The amiable, bearded Bernard King, its founding principal, secured university status for Dundee Institute of Technology in 1994, and continued raising its profile in subsequent years while altering the city centre's profile with a magnificent library, a glass-walled student centre and new accommodation blocks. Among many other ambitious aims, it has pioneered research and development of computer games, harnessing local skills to spin out commercially successful companies. To its barely concealed delight, Abertay was named ahead of Dundee University for teaching in a 2006 *Guardian* survey of the university sector.

Supporting the city's two higher education institutions, Dundee College provides educational shelter to the dispossessed, those without opportunity and those with limited horizons. What the college does best is provide people with aspirational hope. Sure, there are stories of its students making the leap to higher education and becoming graduate stars – but more have learned a vocational trade and now provide a spine of services on which the city's stability depends.

Dundee University is also linked to the medical teaching school at Ninewells Hospital. The 230-acre, south-facing site for the hospital was secured in the 1940s, construction began in the 1970s and the hospital opened with thirty-one wards in 1974. Here, doctors have matched the city's scientists in continuing a wonderful tradition of achievement. I once asked of *Courier* readers, 'When the Big Book comes to be written, what will Dundee be remembered for? The Three Js? Or the three Ms – marmalade, mill girls and missionaries? Or the two Rs – runners Jenny Wood Allen and Liz McColgan?' I also added the three MOs – the missed opportunities of a Ford factory which failed to materialise, the Waterfront shambles and the missing maritime museum. This was at a time when the city was fighting to build the Sensation science centre between Marketgait and Roseangle, and I used the article to bang the drum on Dundee's powerful scientific traditions and achievements.

It was no hard task, listing the likes of Sir James Ivory (1765–1866), mathematician to the king and an eighteenth-century astronomer ranked alongside Newton; Williamina Fleming (1857–1911), the Dundee girl who published a classification of 10,351 stars in 1890 for Harvard University – the first map of the stars; James Bowman Lindsay (1799–1862), a pioneer of electricity and wireless telegraphy, lauded by Marconi; the 'father of planning' Patrick Geddes (1854–1932), a contemporary of Darwin and Ruskin; or indeed, Sir Robert Watson Watt, the radar pioneer whose secret work at University

College Dundee arguably helped shorten the Second World War. Such scientists achieved success in their own field in their own time.

The city's medical pioneers also put Dundee on the map and continue to do so. A remarkable doctor to emerge from the Victorian era at Dundee Royal Infirmary was Thomas MacLagan. MacLagan investigated the causes of rheumatic fever. He looked for plants common to cold, damp places and used effusions of the willow bark (salicin) to treat pain among his Dundee patients. He reported his treatment of rheumatic fever using salicin in *The Lancet* in 1876. At the same time, Felix Hoffmann in Germany was using a salicylic compound to help his father's arthritic pain. When MacLagan died in 1903, *The Courier* commented that he and Hoffmann had 'almost simultaneously discovered the use of salicylic acid for the same purpose, but Dr MacLagan's method of treatment is recognised as superior to the other'. It was Bayer, the company Hoffmann worked for, which in 1899 patented the product as a new drug. It was called aspirin.

Perhaps the most unusual exhibit in Ninewells Hospital's medical museum is the forearm preserved in alcohol of Dr George Pirie (1865–1929). Pirie was aware of Wilhelm Röntgen's experiments in Germany with rays capable of passing through substances opaque to light. Röntgen had given them the name X-rays. In spite of discovering their lethal properties, Pirie continued to devote his working life at Dundee Royal Infirmary to developing X-rays. Tumours and cracks began to appear on his hands. Before long, both hands and the lower half of one arm had to be amputated. Yet Dr Pirie worked on at the Infirmary until 1925.

While Dundee's rich links to medical research have remained in good hands, the Infirmary, after a splendid innings of 200 years, closed in 1998. Since then its principal buildings on Constitution Street have undergone redevelopment to become housing. In a way, the brooding presence of Ninewells always suggested the writing was on the wall for DRI and the relocation of its services inevitable. Yet it was never a clapped-out hospital. It was on the button, firing on all cylinders until the day the last ambulance moved the last patient from its premises in 1998.

A Dundee United-supporting Islay man called Bill Stewart, then chairman of Tayside University Hospitals NHS Trust, put the metaphorical boot into DRI by rubber-stamping its closure. The city could forgive him. Sir William Stewart, as he became after   name-dropping posts such as Chief Scientific Officer to Mrs Thatcher and John Major, chairman of Porton Down research facility and chairman of Tony Blair's inquiry into mobile phones, was the biologist who kick-started the department that put Dundee University and Ninewells on the global science map. Appointed professor of biology at Dundee in 1968, aged only thirty-two, he got into cahoots with the university's first principal James Drever and ignored the government's ruling that Dundee shouldn't develop a BSc in life sciences. Covertly the two island men and adopted sons of Dundee developed one nonetheless.

The baton was passed to Professor Sir Philip Cohen, currently one of the world's top ten cited scientists. Headhunted by leading medical institutions, Cohen has instead remained in Dundee, latterly building up a world-class life sciences team attempting to unlock the fundamental causes of disease. This is now based at the

£13 million Wellcome Trust institute of biomedical sciences in the city's Hawkhill, opened in 1997 and dubbed the city's Citadel of Science. When Cohen arrived as a lecturer in biochemistry in 1971, university academics and medical researchers had a notoriously fickle relationship. Today, Ninewells Medical School is a world-class teaching institution and an integral part of the city's biomedical and life sciences sector, which alone accounts for over 2000 jobs in the Dundee area. A new £23 million Life Centre for Inter-disciplinary Research on the Hawkhill will take this work well into the twenty-first century. The university's school of life sciences recently reached a £100 million milestone in external grants to support the research of the scientists from over fifty countries working on understanding many diseases and conditions, including arthritis, cancer, diabetes, heart disease and stroke. No-one could have foreseen this revolution in preventative healthcare in a city which was once Scotland's worst for overcrowding and disease.

Some of the world's leading scientists have followed Cohen's path to the city, among them Professor Sir David Lane and Professor Sir Alfred Cuschieri. When Cushieri removed an infected gall bladder from a fifty-eight-year-old Dundee housewife at Ninewells in 1987, he made medical history. It was Britain's first ever keyhole surgery operation. Afterwards he developed many of the techniques and instruments used today in the field of endoscopic surgery. He told me once, 'For a long time people thought I was crazy. But I had absolutely no doubts that keyhole surgery was possible.'

He recalled the first operation in Dundee in 1987: 'We did not have monitors. That meant I had to look down a narrow telescope and nobody in the operating theatre knew what I was doing. Only I could see, and this was really very strenuous and stressful.' Currently professor of surgery at Ninewells Hospital Medical School, the Maltese-born surgeon introduced Britain's first training unit for minimal access surgery in Dundee in 1996.

One of the first former DRI facilities to be converted into flats was the red-bricked building fronting Dudhope Street. This unit was opened in 1902 as a cancer treatment ward, by no means the first far-sighted gesture by the jute manufacturer Sir James Caird of Ashton Works. Yet it took a further eighty years before Dundee was back on the map as a dynamic cancer-fighting centre. The modest, brilliant Professor Sir David Lane led the city's cancer crusade. It was Lane who discovered the p53 gene, later known as the Guardian Angel gene, which is involved in about sixty per cent of cancers. For the next twenty years, research on the gene dominated his work, as it has done with the world's top pharmaceutical companies. The breakthrough in Lane's research is part of the city's medical folklore. A pub conversation among a group of Dundee University scientists prompted Peter Hall, professor of pathology, to volunteer to experiment on himself to demonstrate that p53 was a vital human defence system which prevented damage to cells. The simple but painful idea involved Professor Hall rolling up his sleeve and effectively sunburning his arm under an ultra-violet light. Lane, who was only nineteen when his father died from cancer, told me, 'We'd done it in test tubes and tissue culture but it was a very important result to show us that this gene product really is the guardian of genetic material.' One wonders if he will be involved when the twenty-first century finally unlocks a cure for cancer?

While the development of new industries, the arrival

of *Discovery*, university status, world-class research and a transformation in how others see us have all helped to counteract Dundee's manufacturing hangover and dented image, in another respect the city has stood still.

In 1901, the population of Dundee stood at 160,871. Eight censuses and ninety years on, the figure was, remarkably, only forty-three more. But in the fifteen years since the 1991 Census, the city's population has crumbled away to around 140,000 and only now shows signs of stabilising. Loss of population brings significant physical, economic and social consequences. It has implications for inward investment, for attracting economic funding and benefits, and presents problems for planners in terms of schools and nurseries, housing and roads. In 1986, for example, the Tayside Draft Structure Plan proposed that Dundee planned for a population of 178,000 in 1997. It was 30,000 out, the figure at June 1996 being 148,000.

Celebratory millennium fireworks over the Law could not disguise concerns over the town's long-term stability. Part of Dundee's problem has been the fluidity and confusion over its post-war political administration. After local government reorganisation in 1975, Dundee became part of the powerful Tayside Region, which extended from the Drummochter Pass on the A9 to the north, to a point near Kelty to the south, to Greenloaning westwards, to a point north of Montrose in the north-east. With ancient burghs losing proudly-held titles and privileges, the region got off to a bad start. There were disputes about its coat of arms and its official civic car. Perth and Blairgowrie refused to donate links from their provosts' chains towards the new regional chain of office. There was even a dispute over the furniture to be used in the regional council's headquarters, a controversial tower block built on the site of the former Shore Terrace bus station.

But in May 1975, bells rang and after more than 600 years Dundee Town Council ceased to exist. The regional council and the slimmed-down Dundee District Council co-habited in the newly built Tayside House, and much of the public in both town and countryside had no idea who was governing them or which services each authority provided. Whether it was liked or loathed, Tayside Regional Council, usually dominated by Dundee-based Labour councillors, was difficult to ignore. It introduced a lottery, twinned with Charente in France, declared itself nuclear free, trundled out ancient Green Goddess fire engines during a firefighters' strike, and flew the African National Congress flag in solidarity with Nelson Mandela.

Twenty years of it was enough. Come 1995, confused electors had had their fill of the monolith council, and the regional council made way for three autonomous single-tier authorities, including Dundee City Council. The publicity surrounding this round of political gerrymandering claimed it was intended to make local authorities more accountable and responsive to the people they served. The government argued that the advantage of single-tier authorities was that one body would be responsible for all services in its area. Admittedly, most folk did not take to the umbrella role of Tayside Region, and its key function of administering strategic services such as education, social work, roads, housing and police. But curiously, with the downsizing to local level that came about with single-tier authorities in 1995, we still have region-wide policing, water, sewage, health care and roads maintenance, though some are now arm's-length services. The city council, meanwhile, is still divided along party lines, or united by curious political marriages of convenience, while courting unwanted headlines from time to time.

The most controversial local authority action occurred in 1980 when Labour members of Dundee District Council bulldozed through a proposal to twin the city with Nablus, the largest Palestinian town on the Israeli-occupied West Bank. Those behind the twinning included George Galloway, who was then Labour Party organiser in Dundee. Opposition councillors described the Labour group's move as 'a blatant attempt to use Dundee District Council as a platform for their obnoxious policies'. The twinning took a more sinister turn when the mayor of Nablus visited Dundee and said the link was evidence that its people supported the Palestine Liberation Organisation. Shock waves spread across the country. The move was perceived as inflammatory and as 'importing the Middle East problems to Scotland'. MPs at Westminster accused the council of creating a sense of outrage. Tempers flared in the city chambers when Jewish students were prevented from laying a wreath under a Palestinian flag as a protest against the twinning. A Jewish firm severed all links with the city and a 5000-name petition calling for the twinning to be cancelled was presented in Parliament. Although the issue faded as the years passed, councillors of various parties and creeds have continued to lock horns over the arrangement. The council view is that the twinning with Nablus is looked upon in the same way as the links with Dundee's other twins, Orleans (France), Würzburg (Germany), Zadar (Croatia) and Alexandria (USA). Perhaps it was politically motivated, but the Nablus twinning was also a brave initiative which said openly to the world that some people in Dundee were aware of events in the Middle East and that progress towards peace and stability in the region was important to them.

As for ordinary electors, well, in 1975 Invergowrie residents went to sleep in Perth and woke up to find themselves in Dundee District. In 1995 they were earmarked for a transfer to Angus, kicked up a fuss and were returned to Perth and Kinross. Now they are busy fighting off Dundee again.

The confused political administration and our scattered maritime heirlooms summon up a parallel in the city's sporting history. How long can a modestly-sized city with a declining population boast two senior football teams which aspire to honours and European competition? That they share the same street just makes this blinkered own-goal arrangement more astonishing. Having said that, both Dundee and Dundee United have had their day since the war. The former were Scottish champions nearly a half-century ago and reached the semi-final of the European Cup when it was in its simpler, more sensible format. United, meanwhile, participated in the final of the lesser competition, the UEFA Cup, and were Scottish Premier League champions before emulating their rivals to reach the European Cup semi-final. Though the fortunes and finances of the two clubs have fluctuated in recent times, both have their heroes, perhaps Billy Steel as a player for the Dark Blues, and a manager, Jim McLean, for the Tangerines. 'Working with the media has been a wee bit difficult for me,' McLean told me once; one of yours truly's career-high understatements.

Football in a history book? Well, in 2006 Dundee City Council loaned the world's oldest football painting to the *Fascination of Football* exhibition in Hamburg, timed to

199

coincide with the World Cup in Germany. *The Village Ba'
Game*, painted in 1818, is part of a series of the same name
by Alexander Carse (1770–1843), which depict villagers
playing an early version of today's game. The National
Library for Scotland also loaned *Vocabula*, a Latin text-
book written by Dundee's David Wedderburn in 1709,
which contains the first reference to football as 'a passing
game'. Birthplace of Scotland? Birthplace of the beautiful
game?

Athletics is another important arrow in Dundee's sporting quiver. The city boasts a running club in its third
century of competition and a couple of women athletes
who are household names for contrasting capabilities.
Liz McColgan, world champion, world record holder and
Olympic medallist, is the better known. McColgan
evolved into a track star, marathon runner of note, wom-
en's coach, television commentator, fitness centre owner,
one-time chairman of Scottish Athletics and a mother of
five. Her greatest night was in cyclone-hit Tokyo in 1991,
where I was among those cheering her to a world title in
a rain-lashed but memorable 10,000 metres.

Jenny Wood Allen was one of the few runners who
could shift the focus of sporting cameras away from Liz.
When Jenny ran her sixteenth and final London Marathon in 2002, she was ninety. In fact, she had taken on the
twenty-six-mile distance for the first time in Dundee in
1983, aged seventy-one, against the advice of all comers.
Jenny, born in Dundee just before the marathon carters'
strike of 1911, finished in five hours something, then
subsequently knocked an hour off that to set a world best
time for the seventy-plus age group. She became a BBC
favourite and a marathon celebrity. Less well known is
the fact that she was a president of the Toastmistresses

Clubs of Great Britain, a Justice of the Peace, a Conservative councillor for fourteen years and a tireless charity fund-raiser.

Two Dundonians have won and worn Olympic gold medals. In recent times, Dundee-born sailor Shirley Robertson joined a very select cohort of Olympians who have won gold medals at consecutive games. Although her skills were learned on the Solent rather than on the Tay, the city remains justifiably proud of the achievements of this daughter of Dundee. But if ever a sporting star learned his trade in the very heart of his native city, it was the former Dundee butcher's boy Dick McTaggart.

McTaggart went to three Olympic Games as a boxer, a record almost unheard of, won gold at Melbourne in 1956, bronze in Rome in 1960 and was a quarter-finalist in Tokyo in 1964. Scottish champion seven times, British ABA champion five times, European champion, Empire champion, and presumably playground champion during the jute depression when he attended St Mary's Forebank School. McTaggart is arguably the finest amateur boxer Britain has ever produced, counted out only once in 637 official bouts – the 637th. He did not turn professional. He became a rat catcher. The city of Dundee gave him a gold watch, named a sports centre after him, and gave him what he told me was his proudest memory: 'Dundee treated me like a king when I returned with the Olympic gold. Thousands were there when I got off the train. Cheering crowds lined the streets. My family got an open-topped bus to our house in Dens Road. I'll never forget it . . .'

Cheering crowds in mind, it was wonderful to witness the city's Octocentenary celebrations in 1991 and an honour as a journalist to be invited to write *The Courier*'s commemorative Octocentenary book – by which time the decision to replace classified adverts with news on our front page had been taken. The Octocentenary loosely celebrated Earl David of Huntingdon's creation of Dundee as a burgh in the late twelfth century. Eight hundred years on it was marked by a 25,000-strong City Square party and a street carnival with 20,000 participants. For many, the Dock Street gasometer decorated as a birthday cake was the unforgettable moment of madness – but where are all those 'Dundee 800' T-shirts now?

The Octocentenary also acted to remind folk of Dundee's artistic heritage. It has never been shouted from the rooftops, but Dundee used to sell more pictures at its annual art exhibition than either Edinburgh or Glasgow. Throughout its 'three Js' period it was awash with private art collections and knowledgeable patrons. In the 1850s, the flax merchant John Bell inspired other prosperous businessmen to collect art and then lend it to the city, not least among his disciples the former provost James Orchar, who amassed 300 works. In recent times the visual arts were bound up with the names of four men who entered our obituary columns within a short time in the late 1990s. The painters James McIntosh Patrick, David McClure and Alberto Morrocco, and the *Nature Diary* artist and columnist Colin Gibson defined artistic life in the city during the second half of the twentieth century, creating a phenomenal Dundee presence across contemporary Scottish art.

Artists also help us to bridge the years so that we can continue to make the acquaintance of characters with roles in this history. We can meet our lord provosts, merchants, jute barons, surgeons and shopkeepers in portraits at the McManus Galleries. A stained-glass window in the City Chambers shows Alexander Scrymgeour in the 1297 siege at Dundee Castle. Another in the City Churches commemorates Mary Slessor's journey to Africa. The Howff, the most evocative symbol of the people's past, marks the resting place of the likes of Alexander Riddoch, James Chalmers and the flamboyant George Duncan. A statue of the reforming MP George Kinloch looks out over Albert Square, recording that his life ended tragically within a year of his entry to the great Parliament of 1832. Grace Darling's thank you letter to Dundee survives, as does the note of condolence sent by Winston Churchill on the death of his nemesis David Couper Thomson. McGonagall is commemorated in stone on the Esplanade, close to where Mayo Avenue recalls the world aviation record attempt of 1938. Brooksbank Library perpetuates the name of mill poet Mary Brooksbank. Street names recall the discovery of aspirin and the X-ray pioneer Tom MacLagan and George Pirie. The Lily Walker Centre in Ann Street and her old home at Grey Lodge in Wellington Street perpetuate the name of the remarkable social investigator.

Dundee history is a thing of the past, and it is not. It is around us everywhere in the present-day city. No plaques required.

10

2000 to 2006
IDENTITY CRISIS

The past is the past. What does the present tell us about Dundee? What does the future hold for it? We can turn to the influential *Lonely Planet Guide* for 2006 for an impartial view. People, it says, are Dundee's best asset. The city is 'fast losing its depressed, post-industrial image' with a reinvigorated cultural centre and some heavily-marketed tourist attractions. In 2005 the guide praised 'the finest location of any Scottish city' and Dundee was 'definitely worth a stopover'. Back in 2003 the backpacker's bible said that Dundee had re-invented itself as 'a modern financial centre which also flirts with cultural ambition'. And in 2002 the authors praised Dundonians as 'among the friendliest, most welcoming and most entertaining people you'll meet anywhere in the country'.

In terms of image, then, something is working. Dundee has left behind Cockburn's 'sink of atrocity' of the nineteenth century and MacDiarmid's 'grim industrial cul-de-sac' of the twentieth. The hitherto trotted-out stories of post-jute decline, unemployment and community desolation have been set aside in media cutting rooms. Even *The Scotsman*, firmly based in Edinburgh, was forced to concede, 'Dundee has never looked better and is promoting itself with an energy and enthusiasm others could do well to copy.'

That is not to say that critical headlines cannot break through the rebranding process – teenage pregnancy rates have a habit of doing so, also the occasional serious crime, the concrete 'regeneration' mistakes of the 1960s, or the architectural 'vandalism' of the 1980s. In some ways, the gap between the poor and the well-off remains as acute today as it was in the jute era. The ability of people to live together in harmony depends on improved social cohesion and inclusion, and is not improved by extremes of poverty and prosperity in pockets of the city that gave Dundee a bad name a century ago.

Dundee can be proud of recent progress and achievements, however. The signs are encouraging that it has shaken off its negative associations and the malicious tittle-tattle which seldom separated fact from fiction. The depressing Dundee of legend is fading. Even the worst of the concrete walkways have tumbled. But leaving the past behind does not mean that Dundee cannot learn from it. History has a role to play in shaping attitudes, as well as town planning.

Mirroring the flood of immigration two centuries ago, but reversing the twentieth-century movement to new estates, people are returning to live in the city centre. The past has played its part. As construction land has become more difficult to secure, developers rediscovered lost mill interiors and saw possibilities for commercial use and for housing. In 1983 Upper Dens Works was converted to provide seventy-three flats. Three years later Tay Works, the Gourlay Brothers' massive mill, which ceased production in the 1970s, was converted to student accommodation. This was followed by the conversion to housing of part of Camperdown Works, once Britain's biggest jute mill. In the mid-1990s, East Port Works, in the city's Cowgate, became a 100-flat development. Breathing new life into the old town, many of the fifty redundant textile mills which survived to the millennium are earning their keep in our modern environment, while continuing a solid link to the life and times of our forebears. Thanks to such developments, excluded communities are less of a problem today than they were in the 1970s and 1980s.

Curiously, though, the jute palace is almost extinct. The most eccentric of them, the baronial homes built by the Gilroy and Grimond dynasties at Castleroy and Carbet Castle in Broughty Ferry, both fell victim to dry rot, while Farington Hall in Perth Road avoided such an ignominious fate by being burned down by militant suffragettes in 1914. Some swagger houses, such as Northwood in Strathern Road, have been converted into commercial concerns or divided into flats, while a few others remain in private hands.

History also reminds us that Dundee's past was not plain sailing and neither have been her attempts to find successors to jute and electronics. When half a dozen computer games companies located in and around the city in the 1990s, creating a block of expertise and developing such best-selling games as *Grand Theft Auto*, *Lemmings*, *Formula I* and *State of Emergency*, there were hopes that Dundee would have a long-term pivotal role in this important twenty-first-century industry. But maintaining momentum in the face of fierce global competition has seen orders dry up and some of the largest companies go to the non-virtual wall. Elsewhere, a £50 million digital media park in Seabraes Yards, on former railyards west of Dundee station, intended to provide top quality accommodation for high-tech business start-ups, has seen some of its digital-age occupants struggle to survive. Further west, an ambitious MediPark was planned in 2002 to offer health-related companies the chance to develop laboratory and production space on a greenfield site close to Dundee Airport. Despite extensive marketing, its first occupant did not move in until the summer of 2006. So the early 2000s have provided every bit as competitive a challenge as that faced by the faltering linen mills of the early 1800s or the declining jute firms of the 1900s.

Dundee also experienced peaks and troughs when the telephone industry began scouring Britain to locate a revolution in the industry called 'call centres'. From 1990 one call centre a month was established in Scotland, primarily on the back of research which praised the trustworthiness of the Scottish accent. In 1992, the insurance giant General Accident became the first to risk the Dundee dialect, innocently reasoning that half a million Londoners within the M25 orbital ring road would have no trouble understanding 400 folk saying 'see ya ehfter' instead of 'goodbye' in its Technology Park call centre 450 miles away. Another industry giant, Tesco, then opened a call centre at Dryburgh industrial estate, followed by other major companies and an insulting smattering of civil service departments – far fewer than any other city in Scotland, despite years of campaigning. The bubble soon burst. Some call centres have closed or reduced in size, their functions transferred to the Indian subcontinent and other locations. Lessons could have been learned from the city's history. Dundee jute companies found it cheaper to manufacture abroad – as did incomers like Timex.

The news is not all gloomy. Ambitious plans for the waterfront will see Tayside House demolished by 2009 and the City Council moved to new headquarters in North Lindsay Street to be called Dundee House. The central waterfront redevelopment is planned over thirty years and intends to reunite residents with the river. So far, part of South Marketgait has been realigned and the eyesore footbridge leading to the railway station removed. The rail tunnel beneath Tayside House is currently being strengthened to bear a revised street layout. A civic area and marina will be established to the south of the Caird Hall, on the site of the old Greenmarket. Eventually, the Olympia centre, the Hilton Hotel and the casino may join Tayside House in the demolisher's scrapyard. All being well, the Tay Road Bridge ramps will be realigned to make way for a mix of housing, office and leisure use, perhaps allowing the river to be harnessed for broader purposes again.

The debate continues over wider development. Dundee's boundaries are hemmed to the extent that vast peripheral estates are a thing of the past. Annexing the Sidlaws, Monifieth and Invergowrie wards would provide welcome revenue, but would alienate reluctant neighbouring communities and councils. Dundee City Council is prepared for a long haul on the issue, however. In summer 2006, it restated its commitment to lobby to widen its eight miles by six boundaries, and thereby increase its council tax base. The protest of well-heeled, well-connected communities might be too heavy a counterweight against change. The debate over smaller developments – numerous on-off, yes-no, up-down, build-demolish decisions – continues to stall progress, not least when it involves greenery. But at least no one is condemning Dundee for trying. There is a new understanding of how a city must generate income to sustain services.

Further change can be expected if the Scottish Executive drives forward proposals for city region status.

Throwaway judgements remain, and now and again Dundee's character is spread before the public in printed nonsense, not least by central belt-based newspapers, which have a happy knack of ignoring good news from this area while criticising it with less-than-exhaustive research. Nevertheless, the city has re-invented itself across a raft of strengths – as a tourist destination, a centre of educational and technological excellence, a cultural quarter of national importance and a financial hub of the north-east of Scotland. This is supported by a mix of long-established family firms such as D. C. Thomson and food retailers C. J. Lang, incomers like Michelin and NCR, and twenty-first-century industries across the biotechnology, internet services and graphic design sectors.

Modern Dundee boasts buildings that are no longer grim and grey but of the quality and distinction of Abertay's award-winning library and student centre, the Wellcome Building in Hawkhill, Maggie's Centre designed by Frank Gehry at Ninewells, the innovative Bank of Scotland and the elegant Debenhams straddling the Marketgait. There is less room for disparaging comments now – yet the 'wow' factor is woefully missing from hotel and government buildings on prestigious riverside sites.

The city is also rediscovering the will to stage major events – such as the Big Weekend Radio 1 festival in the grounds of Camperdown Park, which welcomed 30,000 pop fans in May 2006. It attracts similar numbers to its Flower and Food Festival, while drawing in thousands of visitors for jazz, guitar and blues festival programmes throughout the year. It loses out, however, to other cities in attracting a fair share of the lucrative conference trade.

Above all, Dundee has rekindled its historic links to the arts through developing a dynamic cultural 'quarter' in the Perth Road area. Dundee Contemporary Arts (DCA), opened in 1999, buzzes near the Rep's third home in Tay Square, alongside a cluster of individual shops, art galleries and the Sensation science centre. Three Dundee-based arts organisations, the theatre, DCA and Scottish Dance Theatre, now attract foundation funding of over £2 million from the Scottish Arts Council, recognising their pre-eminence and international standing. Together these institutions have helped to positively shape attitudes to a city transformed from Scotland's cultural desert into a mouth-watering artistic oasis.

As to the future, so much good comes out of Duncan of Jordanstone Art College that I am embarrassed to leave it so late before turning to it for words of inspiration. Biowoman, a ninety-foot statue of a naked woman, wants to lean nonchalantly against the college building in Perth Road. Biowoman may be kicked into touch, as were previous proposals to illuminate Cox's Stack and the Law for PR purposes, but this grand, ambitious thinking is perhaps what the Dundee of the future requires. After all, the ambitious eighteenth-century town proclaimed its artistic credentials by building a colossal statue of Apollo in Castle Street.

Go for it.

POSTSCRIPT

It is the last day of July. I am writing this from the seat in City Square where this book began. It is lunchtime. Office workers, shoppers, students and parents with children are eating sandwiches and salads under dreamy blue skies and the warm sunshine that has blessed this summer of 2006. Fountains swoosh and leaves swish. Pigeons strut about looking for crumbs. Braithwaite's coffee smell swirls through the air. It is that sort of day. Shirtsleeves, sunglasses, sun cream. As if to show history does not stop, we are sitting on 1000 years of Dundee's past. Under my feet are flagstones. Below that are the foundations of William Adam's 1732 Town House. Below that are the remains of the burgh's earliest Tolbooth on land given by Robert the Bruce in 1327. And beneath that are the stones of St Clement's church and possibly evidence of Dundee's links to the Vikings. A book on history is an ideal way of emerging from the past and giving the old town an identity fit for the twenty-first century.

Enjoy your bit of it.

BIBLIOGRAPHY

Early Period

Boethius, Hector (1526), *Scotorum Historiae*, Paris: no publisher listed.

Defoe, Daniel [1724–7] (1976) *A Tour through the Whole Island of Great Britain*, London: Penguin.

Duncan, A. A. M. (Ed.) (1988), *The Acts of Robert I, King of Scots, 1306–29*, Edinburgh: Edinburgh University Press.

Hall, Derek (2002), *Burgess, Merchant and Priest, Burgh Life in the Scottish Medieval Town*, Edinburgh: Birlinn.

Hay, W. (1886), *Charters, Writs and Documents of the Royal Burgh of Dundee*, Dundee: Dundee Town Council.

Knox, James (1831), *The Basin of the Tay*, Edinburgh: J. Anderson and W. Hunter.

Maxwell, A. (1880), *Old Dundee Prior to the Reformation*, Dundee: William Kidd.

Perry, David (2005) *Dundee Rediscovered, The Archaeology of Dundee Reconsidered*, Perth: Tayside and Fife Archaeological Committee.

Stringer, Keith (1985), *Earl David of Huntingdon*, Edinburgh: Edinburgh University Press.

Torrie, Elizabeth P. D. (1990), *Medieval Dundee, A Town and its People*, Dundee: Abertay Historical Society No. 30.

Wyntoun, Andrew of (1903), *The Original Chronicle of Andrew of Wyntoun*, 3 Vols, Edinburgh: Scottish Text Society.

Middle Period

Anon. (1651), *A Narrative or Diary of the Proceedings of the Forces under Lt General Monck*, London: G.H.

Baxter, J. H. (1960), *Dundee and the Reformation*, Dundee: Abertay Historical Society No. 7.

Blain, William (1946), *Witch's Blood*, London: Hurst and Blackett.

Brown, P. Hume (1914), *The Union of Scotland, 1707*, Glasgow: Outram.

Gumble, Thomas (1671), *The Life of General George Monk, Duke of Abermarle*, London: printed by J. S. for Thomas Basset.

Harrison, William (1587), *Description of England*, London: Bungay.

Lamb, A. C. (1892), *Guide to Remarkable Monuments in the Howff, Dundee*, Dundee: G. Petrie.

Lythe, S. G. E. (1958), *Life and Labour in Dundee, From the Reformation to the Civil War*, Dundee: Abertay Historical Society No. 5.

Mendelson, S. and Crawford, P. (1988), *Women in Early Modern England 1550–1720*, Oxford: Oxford University Press.

Merriman, Marcus (2000), *The Rough Wooings of Mary Queen of Scots 1542–1551*, East Linton: Tuckwell Press.

Millar, A. H., (Ed.) (1898), *The Compt Book of David Wedderburne, Merchant of Dundee 1587–1630*, Edinburgh: Scottish History Society.

Millar, A. H., (1887), *Roll of Eminent Burgesses of Dundee 1513–1886*, Dundee: Dundee Town Council.

Sanderson, Margaret H. B. (1986), *Cardinal of Scotland: David Beaton c.1494–1546*, Edinburgh: Donald.

Slezer, Johannes (1874), *Theatrum Scotiae*, Edinburgh: J. Leake for A. Swalle.

Small, David (1792), *A Statistical Account of Dundee*, Dundee: no publisher listed.

Warden, Alex (1872), *Burgh Laws of Dundee*, London: Official documents (Dundee).

Modern Period

Anon. (Fox, William) (1792), *An Address to the People of Great Britain on the Propriety of Abstaining from West Indies Sugar and Rum*, Dundee: G. Milln and E. Leslie.

Anon. (1999), *Discovering Dundee*, Dundee: City of Discovery Campaign.

Anon. (1932), *Do It At Dundee*, Dundee: Dundee Corporation.

Anon. (1887), *Flax Growing, its Cultivation, Preparation and Profits*, Dundee: W. and D. C. Thomson & Co. Ltd.

Anon. (c.1935), *Mary Lily Walker of Dundee*, Dundee: Dundee Social Union.

Anon. (Brown, William) (1862), *Reminiscences of a Flax-Spinner by a Flax-Spinner*, Dundee: no publisher listed.

Anon. (1833), *The Statistical Account of Dundee*, Dundee: no publisher listed.

Barrow, J., (Ed.) (1952), *The Port of Dundee: Official Handbook*, Cheltenham: Harbour Trustees.

Blair, Norman (2005), *There and Back – No Short Cuts. 1939–1945, A Memoir*, Dundee: private circulation.

Brooksbank, Mary [1966] (c.1982), *Sidlaw Breezes*, Dundee: David Winter & Son.

Brooksbank, Mary [1968] (1971), *Nae Sae Lang Syne*, Dundee: Dundee Printers.

Crawford, W. (1777 and 1793), *Plan of the Town and Harbour of Dundee*, Dundee: E. Leslie.

Dick, William (1820), *Remarks on Epidemic Fever Commonly called Typhus*, Dundee: Alex Colville and Co.

Dickson, A. and Treble, J. H. (1992), *People and Society in Scotland*, Vol II, 1914–1990, Edinburgh: John Donald in association with the Economic and Social History Society of Scotland.

Gauldie, Enid, (Ed.) (1969), *The Dundee Textile Industry 1790–1885*, Edinburgh: T. & A. Constable Ltd.

Gauldie, Enid (1989), *One Artful and Ambitious Individual*, Dundee: Abertay Historical Society No. 28.

Herman, Arthur (2002), *The Scottish Enlightenment*, London : Fourth Estate.

Hume, John (Ed.) (1980), *Early Days in a Dundee Mill, 1819–23*, Dundee: Abertay Historical Society No. 20.

Jackson, G., with Kinnear, K. (1991), *The Trade and Shipping of Dundee*, 1780–1850, Dundee: Abertay Historical Society No. 31.

Jackson, J. M. (1979), *The Third Statistical Account of Scotland: The City of Dundee*, Arbroath: Arbroath Herald Ltd for the Scottish Council of Social Service.

Jeffrey, Andrew (1991), *This Dangerous Menace: Dundee and the River Tay at War*, Edinburgh: Mainstream.

Jones, S. J., (Ed.) (1968), *Dundee and District*, Dundee: British Association for the Advancement of Science.

Leggat, William (1893), *The Theory and Practice of Weaving Linen and Jute Manufacturers by Power Loom, etc*, Dundee: William Kidd & Sons.

Lenman, B., Lythe, S. G. E. and Gauldie, E. (1969), *Dundee and its Textile Trade 1850–1914*, Dundee: Abertay Historical Society No. 14.

McGill, Linda (c.1985), *Dundee's Theatrical Past: Some Brief Notes*, Dundee: Dundee District Libraries.

McGill, Linda (1988), *The Loss of The Steamship* Forfarshire, Dundee: Dundee District Libraries.

McGill, Linda (1995), *The* Mars *Training Ship*, Dundee: Auchterhouse.

McGonagall, William (1890), *Poetic Gems*, Dundee: Winter, Duncan and Co.

McIntosh, James (c.1886), *The Life and Adventures of James McIntosh, the Legless Cyclist, with an Account of his Adventures in the Arctic Regions*, Dundee: John Leng.

Millar, A. H. (1901), *The Dundee Advertiser, 1801–1901, A Centenary Memoir*, Dundee: John Leng.

Miskell, L., Whatley, C. and Harris, B., (Eds) (2000), *Victorian Dundee: Image and Realities*, East Linton: Tuckwell Press.

Miskell, Louise and Whatley, C. A. (1990), 'Juteopolis' in the Making: Linen and the Industrial Transformation of Dundee, c.1820–1850', *Textile History*, 30:2, Newton Abbot: David & Charles.

Murray, J. and Stockdale, D. (1990), *The Miles Tae Dundee*, Dundee: Dundee Art Galleries and Museums.

Paterson, Tony (1980), *Churchill: A Seat for Life*, Dundee: David Winter.

Phillips, David (1981), *The Hungry Thirties*, Dundee: David Winter.

Scott, A. M. (2003), *Dundee's Literary Lives*, Vol. 2, *Twentieth Century*, Dundee: Abertay Historical Society No. 43.

Seymour, Miranda (2000), *Mary Shelley*, London: John Murray.

Stewart, Bob (1967), *Breaking the Fetters*, London: Lawrence and Wishart.

Stiven, W. (1936), *Dundee Old and New*, Dundee: T. M. Sparks & Co.

Walker, David (1977), *Dundee Architecture & Architects 1770–1914*, Abertay Historical Society No. 18.

Walker, William (1979), *Juteopolis, Dundee and its Textile Workers 1885–1923*, Edinburgh: Scottish Academic Press.

Walsh, Lorraine (2000), *Patrons, Poverty & Profit, Organised Charity in Nineteenth-Century Dundee*, Dundee: Abertay Historical Society No. 39.

Warden, Alex (1864), *The Linen Trade, Ancient and Modern*, London: Cass.

Watson, Mark (1990), *Jute and Flax Mills in Dundee*, Tayport: Hutton Press.

Watson, Norman (1991), *The Courier Book of Dundee*, Dundee: D. C. Thomson & Co. Ltd.

Watson, Norman (1997), *Daughters of Dundee*, Dundee: Linda McGill.

Watson, Norman (1990), *Dundee's Suffragettes: Their Remarkable Struggle to win Votes for Women*, Dundee: N. Watson.

Watson, Norman (2000), *The Dundee Whalers*, East Linton: Tuckwell Press.

Whatley, C. A. (1990), *The Remaking of Juteopolis, Dundee c.1891–1991*, Dundee: Abertay Historical Society No. 32.

General Histories

Anon. (Robert Mudie) (1822), *Dundee Delineated*, Dundee: A. Colville and A. M. Sandeman.

Beatts, J. M. (1882), *Reminiscences of An Old Dundonian*, Dundee: Dundee Corporation.

Burton, J. H. (1897), *The History of Scotland*, Edinburgh: William Blackwood and Sons.

Chalmers, James (1842), *The History of Dundee From its Origins to the Present Time*, Dundee: J. Chalmers.

Eunson, E. and Early, W. (2002), *Old Dundee*, Catrine : Stenlake.

Ferguson, Gillian Nicole (2005), *Dundee: A History and Celebration*, Salisbury: Francis Firth Collection.

Kay, Billy (1990), *The Dundee Book*, Edinburgh: Mainstream.

Lamb, A. C. (1895), *Dundee, its Quaint and Historic Buildings*, Dundee: no publisher listed.

Lynch, Michael, (Ed.) (2001), *The Oxford Companion to Scottish History*, Oxford: Oxford University Press.

McKean, C. and Walker, D. [1984] (1993), *Dundee, An Illustrated Architectural Guide*, Edinburgh: Royal Incorporation of Architects in Scotland.

McLaren, James, (Ed.) (1847), *The History of Dundee*, Dundee: J. Durham & Son.

Maxwell, Alexander (1884), *The History of Old Dundee Narrated out of the Town Council Register*, Edinburgh: D. Douglas.

Millar, A. H. (1925), *Glimpses of Old and New Dundee*, Dundee: Malcolm Macleod.

Ogilvie, G. (Ed.) (1999), *Dundee: A Voyage of Discovery*, Edinburgh: Mainstream.

Rollo, James A. (1911), *Dundee Historical Fragments*, Dundee: no publisher listed.

Scott, A. M. (1999), *Discovering Dundee, The Story of a City*, Edinburgh: Mercat Press.

Scott, A. M. (2006), *Dundee: Life in the City since World War Two*, Derby: Breedon.

Sellar, W. and Yeatman, Robert (1930), *1066 And All That*, London: Methuen.

Smith, Robin (2001), *The Making of Scotland*, Edinburgh: Canongate.

Smout, T. C. (1986), *A Century of Scottish People 1830–1950*, London: Collins.

Thomson, James (1829), *The History and Antiquities of Dundee*, Dundee: Robert Walker.

Whatley, Christopher A. (1997), *The Industrial Revolution in Scotland*, Cambridge: Cambridge University Press.

Whatley, C., Swinfen, D. and Smith, A. (1993), *The Life and Times of Dundee*, Edinburgh: John Donald.

Wrightson, Keith (1982), *English Society 1580–1680*, London: Hutchinson.

Yeaman, James (1873), *The Municipal History of Dundee*, Dundee: Dundee Corporation.

Manuscripts and Primary Sources

Anon., *The Crowning of the Steeple*, MS, (private collection).

Calendar of State Papers Domestic, 1650–55, British Library.

Chalmers, James, MS notes and 1822 directory (private collection).

Cox, James, manuscript journal 1808–84, Dundee University Archives.

Duncan, A. A. M., MS notes on Dundee burgh history.

Dundee Social Union (1905), Report on Housing and Industrial Conditions, and Medical Inspection of School Children, Dundee: Dundee Social Union.

Dundee Social Union, committee minutes, 1906–1920, Dundee City Archives.

Dundee Town Council burgess rolls, charters, minutes, Dundee City Archives.

Dundee Town Council New Development Committee minutes, letterbooks and notes, 1947–53, Dundee City Archives.

Dundee and District Jute and Flax Workers' Union, General and Executive committee minute and letter books, Dundee City Archives.

Kinloch, Jean, private correspondence, c.1765, (private collection).

Lamb Collection (various boxes), Dundee Central Libraries.

Lennox, David, (c.1905) *Working-Class Life in Dundee, for Twenty-Five Years, 1878–1903*, unpublished thesis, University of St Andrews Archives.

Murray, Captain John, *The Voyage of the SS* Active *of Dundee*, (private collection).

Scrymgeour, Edwin, Archive Boxes 1–9, Dundee Central Libraries.

Shipping Records, Burgh of Dundee, (various dates), Dundee City Archives.

Suffrage records, Scottish Record Office SRO HH 16/36 and 16/40.

Wanless, John (1833), *The Log of the* Thomas, Dundee Museum & Art Galleries.

Newspapers, Magazines and Journals

The City Echo (1909), Dundee.

The Courier & Advertiser (various dates), Dundee: D. C. Thomson & Co. Ltd.

The Daily Worker (19 March 1993).

Discovery in Scotland (1989, 1993 and 1995) Council for Scottish Archaeology.

The Dundee Advertiser (various dates), Dundee: John Leng & Co.

Dundee Directories, (various publishers and dates).

The Dundee Register (1782), Dundee: T. Colville.

Dundee Yearbook (1870–1916), Dundee: John Leng.

Mill and Factory Operatives Herald (1885–8), Dundee.

The People's Journal (Dundee Edition, various dates) Dundee: John Leng/D. C. Thomson & Co. Ltd.

The Piper o' Dundee (various dates).

Proceedings of the Society of Antiquaries, (various dates, 1750–1850).

Tayside and Fife Archaeological Journal, Vol. 6 (2000) and Vol. 11 (2005).

INDEX